# Eleven Miles to Freedom

The Rock Climbers Guide to Elevenmile Canyon

First Edition

Ben Schmitt

ISBN 978-1-257-78933-7



All maps, topos, and pictures by Ben Schmitt unless otherwise noted.

Cover: The author on *Only Entertainment* (5.13b), the Spray Wall, Elevenmile Canyon.
Keith Ladzinski Photo

# Table of Contents

## WARNING! Read before using this book!

Rock Climbing is an inherently dangerous sport, and serious injury or death can occur. The author, publisher, and all affiliate distributors of this book in no way guarantee the accuracy or quality of the topos, directions, pictures, route descriptions, or fixed protection described. Safety, proper knowledge of the equipment, and a true understanding of your ability are by far the most important factors in climbing, and you as the climber are responsible for knowing how to properly use equipment, understand its limitations, and be able to properly and safely get you and your party up and down climbing routes. If there is any doubt about your abilities or knowledge, don't climb the route or find someone who can teach you the proper techniques, rather than risk killing yourself or someone else.

In the ever changing climate of Elevenmile, weather can be erratic, and bad situations such as a lightning or hail storms can strand you on a route in an instant. Familiarize yourself with the weather patterns and constantly be aware of what is going on around you. As new routes are going up all the time and ethics change, the routes described in this book maybe different from those actually encountered (i.e. anchors missing, new bolts, different bolt count, and different gear). It is your responsibility to adapt to these situations and use your best judgment when climbing a route. Never lower off a single piece, and never take gear for granted.

## Acknowledgments

Anybody who has ever written a guidebook knows that there is no way that anything of this magnitude can come together without the generous and dedicated help of experienced climbers in the community. Their time and effort make the book your holding much more than a flimsy pamphlet of hand drawn topos.

Fundamental to this process are the prolific route developers who have made this canyon what it is today. Without their passion for and dedication to the sport, we would still be climbing the same old choss at the Garden of the Gods. The climbing community in southern

Colorado is surprisingly reticent in giving out information regarding first ascents, and one would think that they would want credit for all the effort and time put into making their routes a reality. Glenn Shuler, Kevin McLaughlin, Brett Peirce, Trask Bradburry, Bob D'Antonio, Stewart Green, and Mike Miller were particularly helpful in providing the information about many of the routes, and I am truly appreciative for their support in this process. Two people in particular deserve special praise, Bill Schmausser and Darryl Roth. Bill for the countless hours spent helping me with pictures, and information, not to mention the years he dedicated toward the modernization of climbing in the Colorado Springs area. Darryl who believed in me from the very get go, and gave me tons on information and priceless stories for the guide (as well as setting the example for how a stoic and wise climber should behave). These two are some of the most unsung heroes of Colorado Springs climbing, and to them I am eternally grateful for the future they created for my generation of climbers.

I have been unbelievably fortunate over the years to have some truly world class individuals as my climbing partners. Special thanks to Scott Hahn, Nathan and Lauren Hollingsworth, Keith Ladzinski, Brett Peirce, Perri Rothweiler, Logan Davis, Eric Morland, Byron Jones, Josh Symes, and Chris Barlow for their donation of time, hardware and undying support for the progression of climbing. I would particularly like to acknowledge Brian Rhodes who constantly helps me with anchor replacement and endured long days of freezing in the cold to get pictures for the book. He also maintains a progressive mindset for the future of climbing. I am truly privileged to have you all as friends!

Finally, my family has been there for me longer than anyone else. I am truly appreciative of my parents Ed and Kerri who have supported me my entire life through my highs and lows, and backed me fully in my goofball endeavors. My father has been my longest climbing partner, and has consistently helped me through my progression in the sport. I am privileged to have shared so many good days on the sharp end with him. Most importantly, I want to thank my beautiful fiancé Emily, who not only unconditionally loves me through the grueling task of writing this book, but spends weeks of her life proofreading and following me through hellish new routing expeditions, braving cold and falling rocks, to support me in delivering a quality final product and giving back to the community in unimaginable ways.

## Introduction

Nestled in the rolling hills behind the sleeping giant of Pikes Peak, this beautiful canyon hosts some of the best climbing in Colorado. Rabbits and deer scamper through the brush. Falcons and blue birds soar overhead. Carried by a cool mountain zephyr, the smell of pine and fresh water drift casually over Indian paintbrush, tickling the trees and sage bushes. This serene mountain setting makes climbing here one of the most enjoyable experiences you will ever have.

The diversity of climbing styles in the canyon is incredible. Hosting splitter Yosemite-like cracks, mind-bending steep sport climbs, techno-slab masterpieces, breathtaking multi-pitch lines, and artistically bizarre blocs scattered over the vast mountain landscape. Established grades range from 5.3 to 5.14, and with the vast potential that still resides, Elevenmile holds a powerful future for the cutting edge of climbing. No matter what your ability as a climber, this special canyon offers something great for everyone. As one of the most family and beginner friendly crags in the country, it's impossible not to have a good experience testing yourself on the gorgeous granite crags that beckon you to climb them!

The history of climbing here is a blend of vague ambiguity and recounted stories from many of the region's hardened pioneers. Technical climbing here seems to have started here in the 1950's and 60's, with members from the Colorado Mountain Club climbing lines on Arch Rock, Pinecone Dome, and Turret Dome as practice for bigger expeditions. Moderate climbs trickled in here and there, but it wasn't until the 1970's that the true potential of the canyon was realized. With Brian Becker as a driving force behind the development, the canyon began to see an explosion in new routes. Pete Gallagher and Peter Williams freed the Teal Tower Route in 1979 and gave Elevenmile its first 5.11. The 19'80s brought another surge in development as Bob D'

Antonio, Richard Aschert, Dale Goddard, Mark Milligan, Mark Rolofson, Neil Canon and Chris Peisker raised the standards yet again. Undeterred by tales that "everything in the canyon has been climbed," these hard men brought the "French" tactics of working routes on rappel, putting bolts in for protection, and making the climbing about the technical difficulty rather than the danger factor. With 35 new 5.12's by the mid 19'80s, Elevenmile was the precursor to the modern sport cliffs like Shelf Road and Rifle. As the development continued through the '90s and the new millennium, local activists like Glenn Shuler, Mark Milligan, Kevin McLaughlin, Mark Vanhorn, Darryl Roth, Dan Durland, Bill Schamusser, Bob D' Antonio, Ian-Spencer Green, and Stewart Green continued to fill in the gaps and round out the canyon, making the special place it is today. With new crags being developed and discovered all the time, Elevenmile is quickly becoming a destination that climbers of all levels can enjoy. There are little tidbits of history for each area, so take your time and tour through Elevenmile's past!

## Getting There

Elevenmile is located 45 minutes west of Colorado Springs off highway 24. From Interstate 25, take the exit for Highway 24 west. Follow this out of Colorado Springs (past Woodland Park and Divide) to the town of Lake George. There are signs near the tackle shop and liquor store pointing towards Camp Alexander and Elevenmile Canyon. Exit left onto Park County Road 96, and follow it for approximately one mile until you see the entrance kiosk on a road leading into the canyon on the right. Take this fork, and pay at the entrance Kiosk. The cost for entry is $5 dollars per day, $45 for an annual pass, and $10 per night for camping. There is a cul-du-sac about 50 feet before the turnoff into the canyon, on your right in the meadow. This is a good place to leave cars and meet people to carpool into the canyon. Mileage for crags inside the canyon will start from the kiosk, so reset your odometer here. Other areas such as Heaven's Gate and Shangri-La are accessed outside the canyon via Forest Service roads (See the map for directions).

## Season

You can climb Elevenmile year round, but the best times to come are late spring, summer, and early fall. South facing crags can be climbed if the sun is out and the weather is 50 degrees or above, but many crags receive snowpack in the winter, and sometimes cracks seep after heavy moisture. Check internet weather sites for Lake George, CO before you go.

## How to Use This Book

**Areas:**

Each climbing area is described so that it can be found easily with its respective maps, pictures, and route descriptions. Each area will have mileage from the kiosk at the entrance to the canyon, as well a parking information. It will also include pictures to denote the following:

 What time of day the sun shines on the walls of the crag.

 The approach time from the parking lot; Difficulty of approach.

 An approach which requires wading the river to get to the cliff.

 Wall orientation.

 The grade range, from easiest to most difficult on the cliff.

Also included in the description of each crag is a tidbit of history or a story about the development for your reading pleasure. Each area has something special and unique to offer, so read the overview and history of the crag before you check them out!

**Routes:**

The core of why you bought this book, here is how it's broken down:

**Traditional routes** This means that you need MOSTLY natural protection (i.e. camming devices, nuts and stoppers, RP's, etc.) to get up the route. I say mostly because many of the routes in Elevenmile are mixed climbs, so that means you may have a bolt on a traditional route but the majority of the protection is traditional gear. If there are bolts, it will be denoted in the protection section of each route. Gear descriptions are also denoted as "gear up to ___inches". Since not everybody uses the same brand of gear, this is meant as a guide to give a reasonable idea of what type of gear to expect. When in doubt, ALWAYS take more gear than you think you will need.

**Sport routes** This means that all you need to get up the route are quick draws. Because many climbs in the canyon are mixed climbs, there may be a couple of sport routes that require a camming unit or two. If this is the case, it will be denoted in the protection section of each route.

Note that not every single obscure route ever climbed in Elevenmile is included in this book. If you do some exploring, you will inevitably find evidence of unreported ascents and ancient pitons long forgotten on some lame 5.8 slab. These routes are not included because A) It is almost impossible track down every single old fogey that has impacted the history of this great area B) The first ascent party does not want to share the information or C) The routes are not good enough to be worth mentioning.

Rather than repeatedly labeling a route "Unknown" if the first ascent information is forever lost in the sands of time (or the inaccessible drug addled depths of some old-timer's memory), I have taken the liberty of renaming routes to give them some reference point other than "That one 5.9." If I have accidently renamed your route, please feel free to contact me with the correct info, and I will happily change it in the next edition.

**Grades:**

All routes in this guidebook are rated using the Yosemite Decimal System. The R or X after the grade denotes how dangerous a route is. R means if you fall, it will likely be a long one and you will probably get hurt. X means if you fall you will hit the ground or die.

Grades are always subjective, and each grade in this book is based on a consensus of the route. They are intended as a ballpark, and should not be taken as set in stone (no pun intended!). If you feel a grade is inaccurate, you are probably a better/worse or taller/shorter climber than I am. Just take climbing as the fun sport that it is, and realize that being outside with friends is much more important than how hard you think you climb.

**Route Description Format:**

/ **Route Name** 5.10a (Y.D.S. Grade) *** (Star quality)

Route description: Where the crux is, what style it is, and any general information. Also interjected are personal opinions, take these with a grain of salt. I have also denoted if you should need a stick clip for safety.

Protection: (cam sizes, etc.) bolt count. Anchor type. (Height in feet)

*First ascent info and year if available (First Free Ascent climber listed first, equippers listed second if it's a sport climb or if it was first aided)*

**Pictures:**

**Stars:**

Each route in this guide has been given a rating based on the star system. These reflect the opinions of multiple climbers, as well as those of the author. This system is here to give you a general feel for a route. You may like it much more or less than is listed, but this should act as a guideline to get you on good routes.

*No Stars* = A bad route! Poor rock quality, bad protection, or just plain dangerous and unpleasant.
*One Star (*)* = Worthwhile outing, but there are better climbs around.
*Two Stars (**)* = A good route, fun climbing or good setting.
*Three Stars (***)* = Great route, one of the best in the canyon.
*Four Stars (****)* = World class climbing, would be popular anywhere!

## Ethics

The truly beautiful aspect of climbing is how uninhibited it is by the rules that govern every other part of society we live in. As the sport grows however, the general guidelines of the community act to preserve the precious and limited resources we as climbers have. Many of these rules should be common sense, but it's still amazing how destructive many people can be if the framework for proper conduct is not spelled out for them explicitly.

The code of conduct is simple: don't steel, don't cheat, and be respectful. Don't steal means that weather it's a bolt, a quick-draw, a piece of fixed gear, or a project that doesn't belong to you, leave it alone! Just because you find something you like does not entitle you to take it, and the phrase "Look, free booty!" is frequently a shroud that all thieves hide behind to justify stealing. Putting up a new route is an incredible amount of work, and the person who spent months working some miserable minimum wage job to buy the drill, bolt gear, hardware, and climbing gear (not to mention the years invested to attaining the necessary skills to climb the route) deserves the chance to get the first ascent. You may be able to onsite their project in oven mitts, but if you need new things to climb, there are thousands of new routes out there for you to put up.

Don't cheat means don't cheat future climbers out of the experiences of climbing that you get to indulge in today. The way we as climbers behave and act today, sets the stage for the future tomorrow. If you put up a route in poor style, are loud and obnoxious at the cliff, act like you own the cliffs, leave trash at the base of the crag, and cause problems, the government won't hesitate for a second to shut down climbing completely.

Be respectful means acting in accordance with that of a decent human being. Smile at everyone you see in the canyon, wave as you pass other cars, be polite, set an atmosphere for success and foster friendliness. No matter how hard you climb, who your sponsored by, how diehard of an ethical position you take, or how radical and cool you and your bros are, realize that in the grand scheme of things all we are doing is climbing rocks, which is maybe the most pointless (and fun!) activity known to man. Do not to take the sport or the summit too seriously.

## New Routing:

The potential for new routes in Elevenmile Canyon is incredible, but proper conduct must be followed before you make an impact on the history of this great canyon. The first question you need to ask yourself is, "Does this route really need to be climbed?" Make sure that the line your about to do is a quality three or four star line, and that it will be enjoyed by future climbers, rather than being a statement of how bold you are. If the line requires bolts for protection (the granite offers many cracks which take good gear; keep that in mind!) make sure to use only the best quality stainless steel 3/8" by 3 ¼" bolts and hangers you can find. Top-rope the route multiple times, get other's opinions, and make sure your bolt placements are in the right spot before you start drilling. Drill ONLY during the off season on weekdays, and don't put up anything that is less than 100 feet from the road. What one person considers cleaning, another may consider chipping, and there is often a fine line between the two. The bottom line is to take the most minimalist approach possible, and realize that the route you establish is a gift to the community that will last forever!

# Table of Climbing Areas

| Crag Name | Number of Routes | Grade Range | Approach | Orientation | Climbing Style | Camping | Quality | Mileage From Entrance |
|---|---|---|---|---|---|---|---|---|
| Heaven's Gate | 14 | 5.9-5.14b | Easy, 10 minutes | West | Sport | Free National Forest | **** | Forest Service |
| Shangri-La | 7 | 5.9 – 5.13d | Easy, 5 min. | North, South | Sport | Free National Forest | *** | Forest Service |
| Guardian Wall | 3 | 5.9 – 5.12b | Difficult, 20 min. | South | Traditional | None | * | 0.2 Miles |
| Knome Dome | 7 | 5.5 – 5.11a | Moderate 15 min. | South East | Sport, Traditional | None | *** | 2.0 Miles |
| Spray Wall | 18 | 5.10d-5.14a | Moderate, 10 min. | South West | Sport | None | **** | 2.1 Miles |
| Bigot Rock | 5 | 5.12a -5.12d | Easy, 2 min. | South West | Sport | None | ** | 2.4 Miles |
| The Tooth | 3 | 5.8 – 5.11d | Moderate, 5 min. | North West | Traditional, Sport | None | * | 2.5 Miles |
| Elevenmile Dome | 10 | 5.5 – 5.11d | Easy, < 1 min. | South | Sport, Traditional, Multi-pitch | None | **** | 2.7 Miles |
| Wildflower Gulch | 5 | 5.7-5.13 | Very Difficult, 20 min. | North West | Traditional, Sport | None | *** | 3.4 Miles |
| Arch Rock | 18 | 5.6-5.11b | Moderate, 5 min. | North West | Traditional, Sport, Multi-pitch | None | **** | 3.7 Miles |
| Turret Dome | 26 | 5.0-5.12b | Difficult, 10-15min. | South West | Traditional Multi-pitch, Sport | None, Picknick area | *** | 4.1 Miles |
| The Sentinel | 5 | 5.9-5.11b | Moderate, 10 min. | North West | Sport | None, Messenger Gulch Picknick | *** | 4.3 Miles |
| Messenger Wall | 13 | 5.6-5.11 | Moderate, 15min. | West | Traditional Sport | None | ** | 4.2 Miles |
| The Sports Crag | 9 | 5.8 – 5.12d | Difficult, 15 min. | South | Traditional, Sport | None | **** | 4.8 Miles |
| Teale Tower | 5 | 5.10c – 5.11c | Moderate, 5 min. | South | Traditional, Multi-pitch | None | ** | 5.0 Miles |
| Springer Gulch | 15 | 5.7 – 5.13a | Moderate, 25 min. | South | Sport, Traditional | Springer Gulch, 15 sites | **** | 5.1 Miles |
| River Wall | 17 | 5.4-5.12c | Moderate, 10 min. | South | Sport Traditional | None | **** | 6.0 Miles |
| **Short Wall** | 2 | 5.10-5.11 | 10 min. Difficult | South | Traditional | None | ** | 6.4 Miles |

| | | | | | | | | |
|---|---|---|---|---|---|---|---|---|
| Spy Roof | 3 | 5.8-5.12c | 5 min. Difficult | West | Traditional | None | ** | 6.6 Miles |
| Indulgence Crag | 13 | 5.9 – 5.12c | Moderate, 15 min. | South | Traditional, Sport | None | *** | 6.7 Miles |
| River Bloc | 4 | 5.10-5.12 | Moderte 20 min. | South West | Sport Traditional | None | ** | 7.3 Miles |
| Cove Rock | 5 | 5.11b – 5.12a | Easy, 3-10 min. | South, West | Sport, Traditional | Cove, 4 sites | *** | 7.7 Miles |
| The Ice-Box | 22 | 5.6 – 5.13c | Easy, 2 min. | West | Sport, Traditional | None | **** | 7.9 Miles |
| Pine Cone Dome | | | Easy, 2 min. | | | None | *** | 8.0 Miles |
| Idle-wild | 9 | 5.10c-5.12b | Easy, 2 min. | Varied, East West | Traditional, Sport | None, Picknick | * | 8.1 Miles |
| Camp Rock | 4 | 5.6-5.10b | Easy, 1min. | South | Traditional | None | * | 8.3 Miles |
| Baboon Rock | | 5.8 – 5.13c | Moderate, 10 min. | South East, South West | Traditional, Sport | Spillway, 15 sites | *** | 8.3 Miles |
| Corridor Crag | 5 | 5.9-5.11c | Moderate, 15 min. | West Facing | Traditional | Spillway, 15 sites | ** | 8.3 Miles |
| Icicle Slab | 2 | 5.10b-5.11b | Moderate, 15 min. | South Facing | Traditional | Spillway, 15 sites | * | 8.4 Miles |
| The Fortress | 10 | 5.9 – 5.12b | Difficult, 25 min. | South | Traditional, Sport | Spillway, 15 sites | ** | 8.6 Miles |

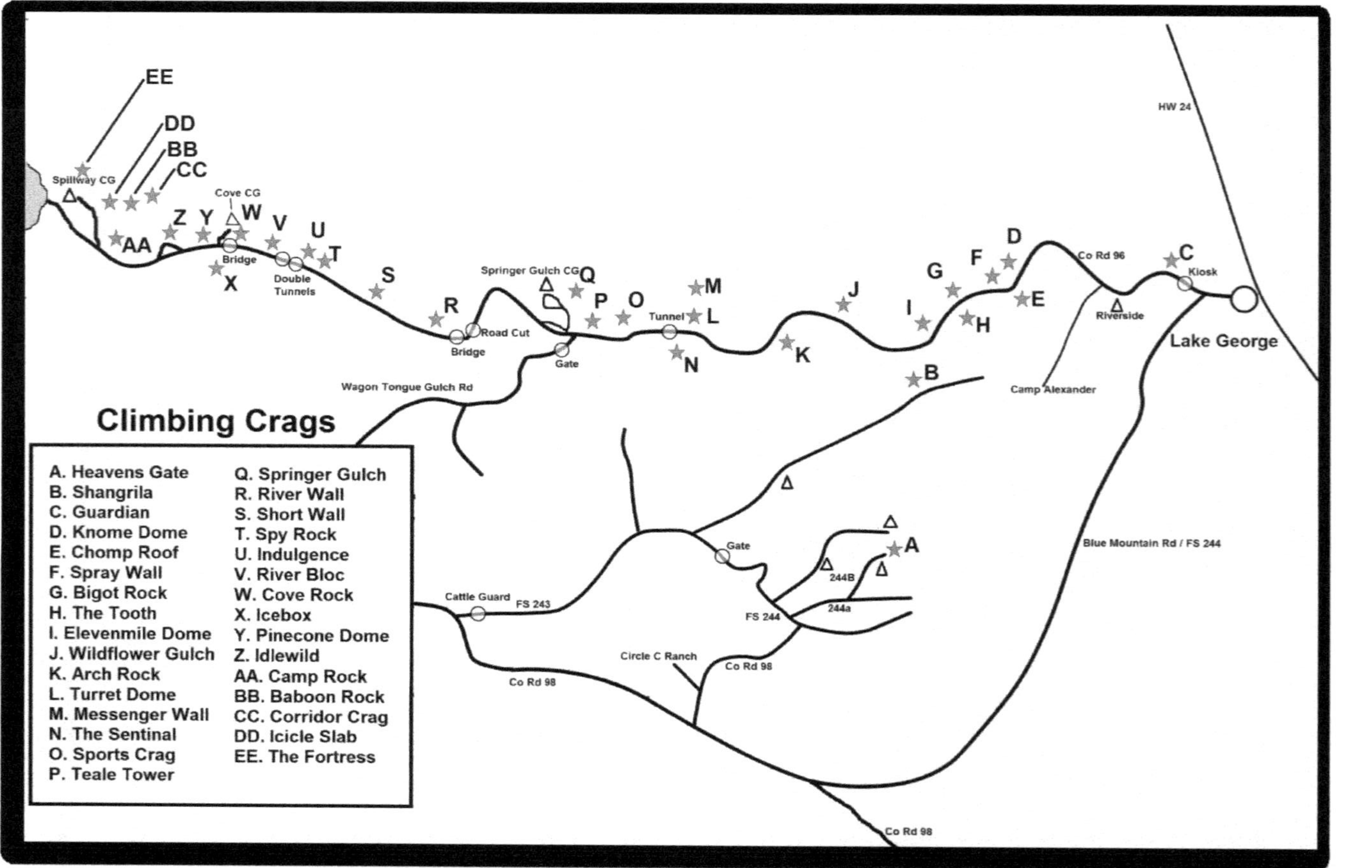
Climbing Crags
A. Heavens Gate
B. Shangrila
C. Guardian
D. Knome Dome
E. Chomp Roof
F. Spray Wall
G. Bigot Rock
H. The Tooth
I. Elevenmile Dome
J. Wildflower Gulch
K. Arch Rock
L. Turret Dome
M. Messenger Wall
N. The Sentinal
O. Sports Crag
P. Teale Tower
Q. Springer Gulch
R. River Wall
S. Short Wall
T. Spy Rock
U. Indulgence
V. River Bloc
W. Cove Rock
X. Icebox
Y. Pinecone Dome
Z. Idlewild
AA. Camp Rock
BB. Baboon Rock
CC. Corridor Crag
DD. Icicle Slab
EE. The Fortress
HW 24
Lake George
Kiosk
Co Rd 96
Riverside
Camp Alexander
Springer Gulch CG
Tunnel
Road Cut
Bridge
Gate
Double Tunnels
Cove CG
Spillway CG
Wagon Tongue Gulch Rd
Blue Mountain Rd / FS 244
244B
244a
FS 244
Cattle Guard
FS 243
Circle C Ranch
Co Rd 98

Graham Espenlaub on *Frozen in Time* (5.12a) at the Icebox. Bill Schmausser photo.

# Heavens Gate

 P.M.  5-10 min.  South West  5.9-5.14

Tucked away in the lush rolling hills to the south of Elevenmile Canyon proper, Heaven's Gate is a true climber's paradise. The rock here is a supreme variety of patinas, slopers, and beautiful edges, which rank as some of the best in the South Platte. The majority of the climbing here is wickedly overhanging granite, with no approach more than ten minutes from the parking.

The area has always been a favorite of Boy Scout groups and weekend warrior campers who come out to ride ATV's and target practice, but it wasn't until Lauren and Nathan Hollingsworth discovered the crag in 2010 that the true climbing development began. As a true testament to their generous and admirable character, Nathan and Lauren drew up directions, encouraged others to come develop, and added some fine additions of their own to the number of classics here. Ben Schmitt, Brian Rhodes, Scott Hahn, Perri Rothweiler, and Logan Davis hit the crag with force over the summer of 2010, and thus, *Heaven's Gate* was born.

**Approach:** Take Co Rd 96 out of Lake George (which turns into FS 244 past the fork which leads to entrance of the main Canyon), all the way around Blue Mountain where it rejoins Co Rd 98 at a large fork. Continue up the small hill, and turn right at the white sign labeled "Circle C Ranch", and take the right fork on to Forest Service Road 244 (The left fork leads to the Circle C Ranch). Follow this for 0.4 miles, cross a seasonal puddle, and turn left immediately after that onto Forest Service Road 244 A. Go 0.1 miles (past a good camping spot on the left), and turn right onto Forest Service Road 244 A for 0.2 miles, through a meadow where the road splits for 40 feet then rejoins, and turn left on 244 B. Continue up the hill for 0.5 miles to where the road dead ends at a cull-du-sac and the parking for the crags. If there is someone camping there, you can park off to the side of the road and walk up to the Emerald Isle and skirt back down, just make sure to give the campers a wide berth and be polite in any interaction.

# The Emerald Isle

With a brief approach directly uphill from the parking lot, this crag has the most variety of the three cliffs and offers a quick workout for climbers who have a limited time to visit.

*From the parking area, head directly uphill through two large boulders, angle left, then switchback right, to a brief scramble up some low-angle rock to the cliff. The first route you will see is Morass Supreme on the large overhanging boulder. Head left along the cliff line to the overhanging alcove. Routes are listed from left to right…*

**A. The Happy Pier** *5.11b* ***

The first route in the Isle, this diverse overhanging line takes two bolts up the overhanging dihedral to a crux move up and left over the lip bulge. Finish with pumpy overhanging climbing up and right to an anchor just right of the big roof.
7 bolts. Lower-off anchors. (50 feet)
*Ben Schmitt and Brian Rhodes '10*

**B. TheRapist** *5.11c* **

Start right of *Pier* off a pointed boulder, and follow a slab up to a roof. Here lies the dynamic crux (a big throw to a good jug) which finishes with easier slab climbing to the anchors.
6 bolts. Open Shut Anchors. (50 feet)
*Re-bolted and fixed by Ben Schmitt '11*

**C. Laura's Arette** *5.9* *

Begin 20 feet right of *TheRapist,* and climb the technical, slabby arête with a committing crux near the last bolt. It would be better if the crux move was not so much harder than the rest of the route. Cool position and a good warm-up!
6 bolts. Chain Anchors. (50 feet)
*Brian Rhodes '10*

**D. Adult Supervision** *5.10a* **

An interesting slab adventure over a variety of intricate features, start ten feet right of *Laura's Arête,* and smear up and right through a crux at the third bolt followed by easier climbing to hidden anchors over the lip.
6 bolts. Chain Anchors. (55 feet)
*Bill Schmausser and Ben Schmitt '10*

**E. Ground Bound Hounds** *5.11c* ***

A cruxy and delicate slab start (recommended stick clip!) climbs up and right through gorgeous stone over a bulge and long (but very easy) run-out which can be protected with a 1" cam, leads to dynamic moves on the steeper panel. Really good slab climbing!
4 bolts, 1" cam. Chain Anchors. (60 feet)
*Ben Schmitt and Ed Schmitt '11*

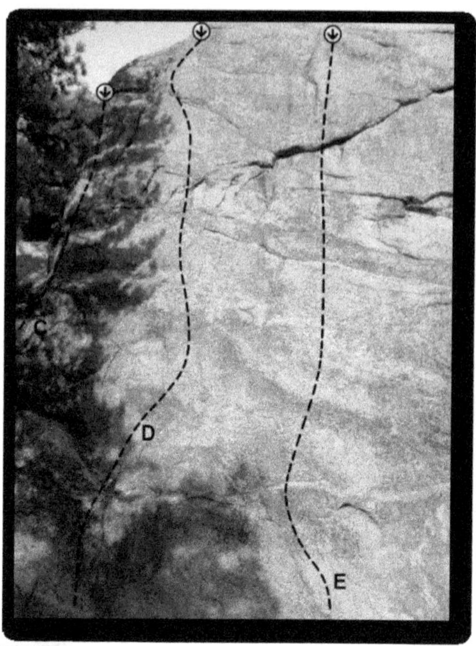

*On the large boulder lying against the main cliff....*

**F. Quisling** *5.12b***

Residing on the north face of the overhanging small boulder, this 3 bolt gem is a beautiful power-endurance crimp-fest over a seemingly endless series of crimps. Cryptic climbing!
3 bolts. Chain anchor. (30 feet)
*Re-bolted and fixed by Ben Schmitt '10*

*Around the corner, in a small alcove between the two large boulders…*

**G. Total Devastation Project** *5.14b* ****
Powerful, thin, and continuous, this gorgeous overhanging beast takes the belly of the bulge through two devious V10 boulder problems up immaculate patina edges. Soft for the grade, but still hands down one of the hardest in Elevenmile!
7 bolts. Cold Shut Anchors. (45 feet)
*Ben Schmitt '10*

**H. Morass Supreme** *5.12a****
Clip the first bolt of *Total Devastation,* and fire up and right through a panel leading to a series of crimps, jugs, and slopers. The crux hits 1/3rd of the way through the route, and gets progressively easier toward the top. Stellar position!
5 bolts. Chain anchor. (40 feet)
*Re-bolted and fixed by Ben Schmitt '10*

# Inception Wall

 **P.M.**  **5 min.**  **South West**  **5.11-5.13**

The first wall to be developed at Heaven's Gate and for good reason. This wickedly overhanging boulder looks easy and featured from the ground, but actually demands an amazing amount of power and precision to scale its sloper filled walls. Don't miss *Inception* one of the best 5.13's in the region!

*Walk from the parking area down the hillside through two large boulders, then hug the ridgeline on the East side of the valley for 300 feet until the wall is visible on the right. There is a faint trail to follow, but if you just traverse the middle of the hillside you should be fine.*

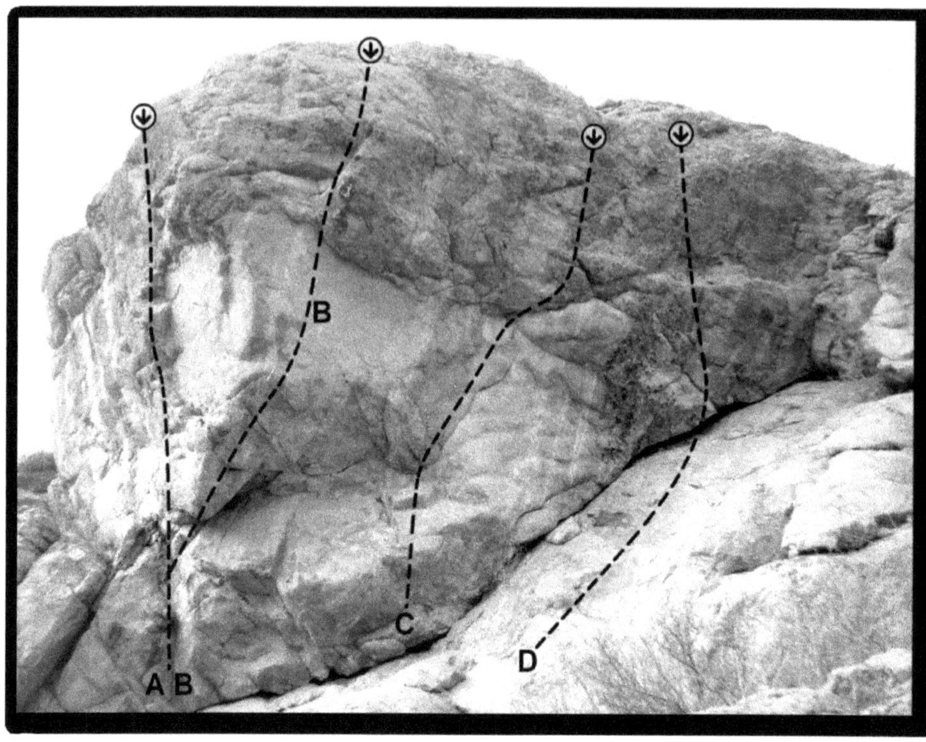


**A.** **Inception** *5.13c* ****

One of the best of the grade in the canyon, this superb 45 degree overhanging route is a beautiful power endurance test-piece that just keeps coming at you! Each move is gradually more difficult than the last, leading to a desperate under-cling crux at 2/3 height.

7 bolts. Lower-off anchors. (50 feet)

*Ben Schmitt, Scott Hahn, Brian Rhodes '10*

**B.** **Open Project 5.13+** **

Begin 5 feet right of *Inception*. Power through a dynamic boulder problem, which gives way to 5.11 climbing to high anchors over the bulge. Absolutely stellar position and decent climbing make this a worthwhile outing.

6 bolts. Chain anchors. (55 feet)

*Ben Schmitt '10*

C. **Closed Project** *5.13+* ***

The well protected angling crack will yield a desperate route when completed. Nathan spent a lot of time bolting this, so he definitely deserves the time to send it! Desperate climbing up the flaring, right trending seam to the bulge where difficulties ease. Angle up left to anchors left of the water groove.
8 bolts. Lower off anchors. (50 feet)
*Nathan Hollingsworth '10*

D. **After School Special** *5.12c* *

Take the easy low-angle slab from the same belay as *Project* and crux up through a small boulder problem past two bolts to a rest. Take 2 more bolts up and right to anchor. The climbing on the panel is good, which makes this route worthwhile.
4 bolts. Chain anchor. (35 feet)
*Ben Schmitt, Logan Davis, and Perri* Rothweiler *'10*

# The Plebian Wall

Hosting a fine assortment of moderates, this beautifully black and green streaked wall offers an assortment of grades akin to, but much more welcoming than, *The Spray Wall* in the main canyon. With routes from 5.10 to 5.13-, there are multiple opportunities for everyone to have fun climbing over a variety of interesting features, as well as enjoy some spectacular views!

A. **Intercontinental** *5.10c* ****

This stellar line takes the center of the detached pillar forming a small cave on the left side of the cliff. This beautiful line incorporates a variety of technical moves on bullet hard stone. Very photogenic, and sustained the entire way!
6 bolts. Chain anchor. (45 feet)
*Ben Schmitt and Peri Rothweiler '10*

*The next four routes are accessed via a scramble up the fixed line through a hole in the back of the cave…*

B. **Alley Cat** *5.11c* ***

The farthest left line on the main cliff. Start directly off the flat platform in the shady alley, and angle up and left through satisfying powerful moves on good crimps and jugs to finish in the pods up top.

4 bolts. Cold-shut anchor. (30 feet)

*Brian Rhodes '10*

C. **Lauren's Overhang** *5.11b* ***

Start just above the left side of the traverse line, and make big moves between decent holds up to the start of a crack. A perplexing crux (with a slight run-out), leads right to anchors.

4 bolts. Lower-Off Anchors. (35 feet)

*Lauren D. Hollingsworth '10*

*Take the fixed line right across the ledge, and belay from the anchors for the next two routes, or use the direct start of Buddha Belly…*

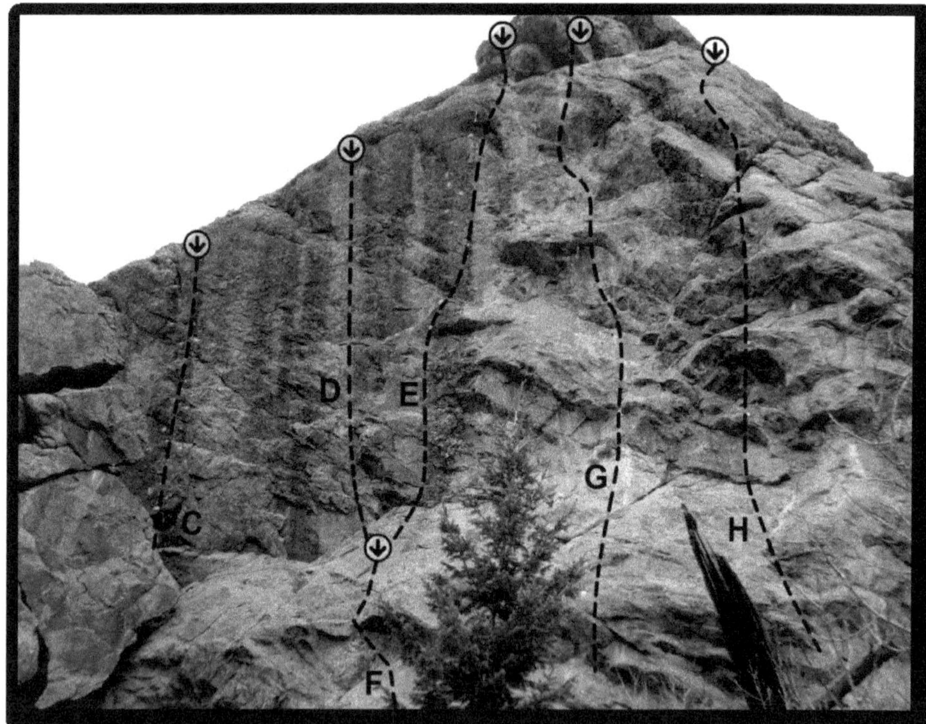

D. **Arco Arena** *5.12b* ***

Start off the anchors at the end of the traverse line, and take the left line of bolts up the beautiful overhanging wall, through jugs (which turn to crimps) to a powerful crux that guards the anchors. Short, pumpy, and classic!

5 bolts. Lower-off anchors. (45 feet)

*Ben Schmitt '10*

E. **Shotgun Piñata** *5.12c* ****

Similar in nature to *Arco Arena* but much more sustained! Angle right off the belay through an endless sea of crimps, to a high dynamic crux at 3/4 height. One of the top three 5.12's at Elevenmile, and has been heralded as one of the best in southern Colorado!

6 bolts. Lower-off anchors. (45 feet)

*Ben Schmitt '10*

*Starting from the ground, the next three routes are listed from left to right…*

F. **Buddha Belly** 5.12d *

A brief, powerful, and height dependent boulder problem through the "belly" of the overhang. Either end at the traverse line anchors, or continue up *Arco* or *Shotgun* for the link-up routes *Buddha's Arena* (12d) and *Buddha's Shotgun* (13a).

2 bolts. Cold-shut anchor. (25 feet)

*Ben Schmitt '10*

G. **Fourier Transform** 5.13a **

Interesting technical climbing through tiered overlaps characterize this deceptively easy looking route. A difficult onsite due to cryptic beta, and is especially deceiving at the crux below the last bolt.

8 bolts. Lower-off anchor. (55 feet)

*Ben Schmitt '11*

H. **Nathan's Arête** 5.12a *

Interesting dynamic climbing through multiple overhangs leads to an awkward technical crux up high on the slab. Finish at anchors right over the lip.

7 Bolts. Lower-off anchors. (60 feet)

*Nathan Hollingsworth '10*

# Shangri-La

 **P.M.**  **5 min. Easy**  **South East / North West**  **5.9-5.13**

It is truly amazing what can be found around the next corner with a little bit of dedication and exploring. Shangri-La is the result of local activists taking initiative and scouting for new areas. Found and equipped in 2008 by Ben Schmitt, this area offers a little something for everyone with every route being put up with the highest quality gear, and with the intention of being a secluded, tranquil, and special place for all those who visit.

**Approach:** Originally this crag was approached by hiking from the pullout 300 feet west from Elevenmile Dome, wading the river, and hiking up Sledgehammer Gulch to the cliff on the eastern hillside. However, with a 4-wheel drive high clearance vehicle, a better approach is done using Forest Service Roads. Approach as for Heaven's Gate, but instead of turning right on 244a, continue on FS 244 which turns into a steep 4WD trail that leads to a meadow. Head through the gate, and take your first right on FS 245. Continue on this for about 1.3 miles to park in a small aspen grove. From here, walk west down the ravine, turn right to hug the hillside after about 300 feet, and the cliff will be visible on your right.

## The Tranquility Wall

 **P.M.**   **5 min. Easy**  **North West**  **5.12-5-14**

*On the overhanging, northwest facing wall…*

**A.** **Rise Over Run** *5.12d* **

Engaging arête climbing, technical dihedral, and a full on campus over the roof characterize this multilevel beast. An in-situ draw on the seventh bolt allows for a safe clip during the perplexing, inverted crux. Hard and deceptive, this one might feel a bit weird until unlocked.

8 bolts to lower off's, (45 feet)
*Brian Rhodes and Ben Schmitt '09*

**B.** **Open Project** *5.14* **

Powerful, sustained, and utterly classic bouldering over bad slopers and worse feet; this savage route tackles two back-to-back V-double-digit boulder problems on slopers to finish up a 5.10+ run-out to the chains. When completed, it will be one of the hardest in the canyon.

6 bolts. Lower off anchors. (50 feet)
*Ben Schmitt '10*

C. **Fight or Flight** *5.13d* ****

The best route at the crag, and one of the best in of its grade in Southern Colorado! A hard and technical slab start (stick clip the first bolt) leads into a power endurance marathon crux up the hanging "refrigerator" with a fight (or flight!) all the way to the chains! A soft 13d variation has been done starting on the right crack and linking into the rest below the overhang using medium sized cams.

11 bolts. Lower off anchors. (60 feet)

*Scott Hahn, Ben Schmitt, Brian Rhodes '09*

D. **Open Project** *5.14-* **

A moderate and terrible chossy start past four bolts gives access to an incredible long dynamic boulder problem up the hanging arête on the right side of the wall. Fantastic position comprised of big moves, technical jessery, and a brutally thin finishing crux ends at the 2 foot long chains.

8 bolts. Lower-off anchors. (55 feet)

*Ben Schmitt '10*

E. **Open Project** *5.12+* *

Start as for *Open Project*, but head straight up to a no hands rest. The climb can end here at the cold shuts (5.11c), or continue up through a crimpy, chossy boulder problem past the seams to an easy dihedral finish. A long route next to the tree!
10 bolts. Lower-off anchors. (60 feet)
*Ben Schmitt '10*

*On the small boulder on the far right side of the wall…*

F. **Girlfriend Route** *5.11c* **

This little gem is located on the small overhang on the far west side of the crag. While this route may be short, it packs a punch! Steep, thuggish climbing on overhanging slopers. The "Girlfriend" this route was bolted for must be mutant strong!
3 bolts. Lower-off anchor. (20 feet)
*Nathan and Lauren D. Hollingsworth '10*

# The Invitation Tower

*On the Tower forming the north side of the canyon…*

G. **Emmows** *5.10a* **

This quality route starts with an excellent crimpy problem up a well protected panel of stone. Then easy fun moves to the anchors at the bulge!
5 bolts. Cold-shut anchors. (30 feet)
*Chris Barlow and Ben Schmitt '10*

H. **The Invitation** *5.9* ***

A technical, crimpy start weaves up and right past two bolts to a no-hands ledge. Follow enjoyable slab crimps all the way to cold shuts at the top of the tower. This is a really well protected climb, with great moves on even better stone!
7 bolts. Cold-shut anchors. (45 feet)
*Kurt Ross and Ben Schmitt '09*

*Starting on the arête around the corner, left of the big tree…*

*I.* **Golden Staircase** *5.10b* *

Hard start surmounting the bulge leads to incredible position up the arête! Good climbing with a hard crux down low over a bulge on the boulder, leads to much easier 5.7 climbing above. Needs re-bolted.
7 bolts. Cold-shut anchors. (60 feet)
*Micah Holt and Ben Schmitt '09*

J. **Ben's Lament** *5.12a* *

A jumpstart off the boulder leads to interesting, powerful climbing to a hand jam crux. Angle up and left through powerful climbing to anchors over the lip. Named for the fact that Ben bolted most of these climbs, but gave away most of the first ascents on them!

4 bolts. Cold shut anchors. (25 feet)

*Chris Barlow and Ben Schmitt '10*

K. **Green Eyes** *5.13a* **

Start on the far left side of the tower, and follow the super steep overhang up and right to a powerful slapping crux at the bulge. Easier moves lead to anchors over the lip. Great position, if only the rock was better!

5 bolts. Chain anchor. (30 feet)

*Ben Schmitt '10*

Brian Rhodes on *Only Entertainment* 5.13b. The Spray Wall. Byron Jones Photo.

# Guardian Wall

*[Located on the North side of the river at .2 miles…]*

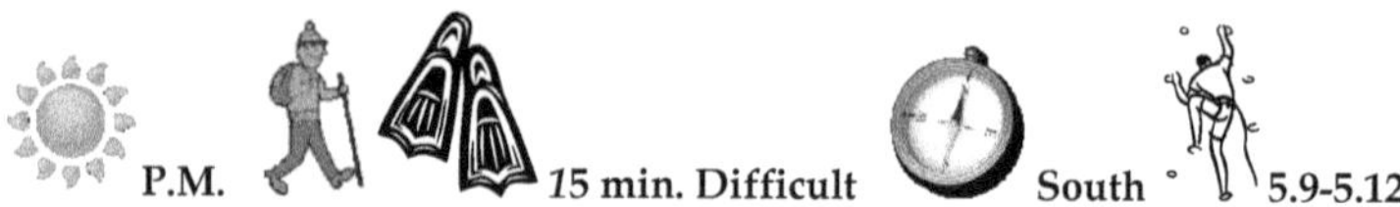


Perched on the hillside guarding the entrance to the canyon, this proud overhanging feature is usually the first thing that catches climber's eyes as they enter into the canyon. With a long approach and only a couple of routes, this is a seldom visited area despite how obvious it is. Most of the routes here are attributed to Bob D'Antonio, Will Gadd, and Brent Kertzman .

**Approach:** To get to the wall, park at the pullout right before the yellow "Narrow Road" sign at .4 miles. Wade across the narrow part of the river here, head up the hillside, over the top of the large cliff and cross the large ravine heading towards the overhanging cliff on the hill side. There is no trail (a tribute to the walls popularity!) so use your best judgment on finding the wall.

A. **Dakota Swing** *5.11c* *

On the far left side of the crag, this route starts left and traverses a seam past one bolt through the technical crux to converge in the dihedral. Steeper climbing through the gradually widening crack takes you to the summit.

Doubles nuts and cams to 2″. No anchor. (40 feet)

*Bob D' Antonio and Brent Kertzman '84*

B. **Dakota Swing (Direct)** *5.12b* *

This hard, thin, and steep bulging finger crack can be linked into the top part of *Dakota* to yield a good line. Essentially a painful boulder problem, you might want to tape up for this one.

Double nuts and cams to 2″, emphasis on finger sizes. No anchor. (45 feet)

*Bob D' Antonio '84*

C. **Mind Games** *5.11c R* *

Difficult climbing up the right trending under-cling seem. Finish up *Secret Journey*. With the marginal rock quality, poor placements, and hard moves, this route is not recommended.

Double nuts and cams to 3″. No anchor. (80 feet)

*Dale Goddard and Will Gadd '84*

D. **Secret Journey** *5.9* *

This worthy route ascends the obvious flaring dihedral system on the right side of the crag. Good protection and fun features make this an enjoyable experience.

Double nuts and cams to 3″. No Anchor (80 feet)

*Brent Kertzmen and Dave Bower '85*

# Knome Dome

*[Located on the North side of the river at 2.0 miles...]*

This is the first crag in the canyon offering reasonable access and moderate climbing, and is often the first stop for intermediate climbers who want an escape from the crowds. With beautiful sunny slabs, close access to the river, and well protected pitches, it's a fine place to take the kids and enjoy some of the best easy routes in Elevenmile.

**Approach:** Park just past the first bridge, ¼ mile upstream of the Water Dome at the Spray Wall Parking area on the right. Take the well traveled climbers trail up the hill, over the ridge then down past the Spray Wall's overhanging sport climbs. Follow the river downstream past a small cave to the dome.

A. **Waterslide** *5.8* **

On the left side of the dome, this route takes the thin, technical slab through a low crux to a sustained seam. Good rock and nice position.
7 bolts. Chain anchor. (65 feet)
*Bill Schmausser and Britt Anderson*

B. **Sleeping Beauty 5.7** ***

Beautiful sustained edging up a long slab to a crux at the horizontal roof. Superb moves on this slab classic.
8 bolts. Chain anchor. (80 feet)
*Bill Schmausser and Britt Anderson*

C. **Heels over Heads** *5.10b* **

In the center of the face, this historic line was the subject of a lengthy and pointless controversy over its retro bolting, but is a better route now that it is no longer a death solo. Angle in from the left past two bolts through easier climbing to join a third and pull over the crux roof. An additional pitch can be linked to the top of the dome, but the first pitch is the most worthwhile.
3 bolts, cams and nuts to 3″. Chain anchor. (80 feet)
*Pete Gallager and Peter Williams '79*

D. **River Madness** *5.11c* **

This direct start to *Heels Over Heads* takes two bolts of vicious technical smearing to join *Heels* at the third bolt. Follow the crack over the lip red point crux to anchors.
3 bolts, cams and nuts to 3″. Chain anchor. (80 feet)
*Bill Schmausser and Britt Anderson*

E. **Water Babies** *5.11a* ***

Good, technical smearing over hard moves which get easier as it angles right to shared anchors with *Tourists and Fisherman.*
4 bolts. Chain anchor. (60 feet)
*Stewart Green*

F. **Tourists and Fishermen** *5.8* ****

Angle up and right through an ultra shallow dihedral to a crux move up left to finish on a nice slab with shared anchors under the roof. Popular, well protected, and quality!
6 bolts. Chain anchor. (60 feet)
*Bill Schmausser*

G. **The Bloody Nit** *5.7*

Uninspiring traditional route which follows the right facing dihedral right of *Tourists* up and over the lip to a bushy 5.4 section. Rappel from the tree.
Cams and nuts to 3". Tree Anchor. (85 feet)
*Larry Schubarth, Robert Karolick, and Bob Somonette '73*

H. **Kiddo Climb** *5.5* ***

Awesome Beginner slab which leads up the right side of the cliff. Well protected and sustained movement to obvious anchors in the overhang.
8 bolts. Chain anchors. (45 feet)
*Bill Schmausser and Britt Anderson*

*Although not part of the Knome Dome, A single route up the overhanging roof is worth mentioning. Chomp Roof is located at 2.1 miles, on the south side of the road across from Knome Dome. Park in the pullout, and head east uphill for 150 feet and the obvious splitter out the roof will be visible…*

A. **Chomp Roof** *5.12a* **

Climb a brief 5.8 approach pitch and traverse the ledge to build a belay below the overhanging roof crack. Launch off the ledge, and fight your way through flaring off-width climbing to build a belay on the summit.
Cams to 4". No Anchor. (70 total feet)

# The Spray Wall

*[Located across the river on the north side of the road at 2.1 miles]*

"Oh yes, about those mind bending steep crags…" is how Darryl Roth, the wall's pioneer developer, first referred to the Spray Wall in an old issue of rock and ice. Roth was blown away by the wall's potential for development, and quickly spread the word about this incredible overhanging crag. Everyone he talked to dismissed it saying, "It's impossible for anything like that to exist in the South Platte, it's all cracks and slabs!" It wasn't until 1994 that Darryl enlisted the help of Dan Durland to start equipping the crag and ultimately create some of the most enjoyable routes on the Front Range.

Later Bill Shmausser, Mike Johnson, and local hard man Ian-Spencer Green came along to fill in the rest of the wall. In 2009, Elevenmile's standards were upped again with another 5.13d and the canyon's first 5.14. Outré Salvo was a ten year project that was the culmination of multiple climbers' efforts. This route, like many others in the canyon, is an example of how powerful climbers can be when they work together to establish futuristic routes and set new standards.

While there has been harsh criticism toward the ethics involved in creating these routes, it's important to understand their place in history as well as the era in which they were established. Climbing is an ever evolving sport, and today more than ever it has changed to focus on high end climbing with minimal impact. The result of all of this, however, is Elevenmile's best steep and user friendly sport climbing crag on pristine bulletproof granite. Climbing this crag is a rite of passage for many local climbers who are breaking into the upper echelon of difficulty. With close proximity to the river and five minutes' walk from the car, this crag offers the some of the hardest climbing in Elevenmile Canyon with 85% of the climbing here rated 5.12 and up. Enjoy!

**Approach:**

The Spray wall is located 1.6 miles from the kiosk on the right side of the road. Drive past the wall, which will be visible on your right, and head over the first bridge to a pullout just past the bridge. Park here, and take the climbers trail that cuts up the hillside east, over the hill, and back down to the wall. *Spray* will be the first route encountered off the trail.

**A.** **Spray Direct** *5.12d ***

The direct start to spray, stick clip the bolt underneath the big under-clings and power your way through small crimps straight up the powerful V6 boulder problem to join Spray and traverse left to anchors. Stick-clip the first bolt.
5 bolts. Lower-off anchors. (30 ft)
*Darryl Roth*

**B.** **Spray** *5.13c* ***

This power endurance route traverses the entire left side of the spray wall via long moves, powerful sapping core tension, and a final crux lunge to a large jug at 3/4 height. No move is harder than V5, but compounded this route packs a huge punch! The boulder behind you is close, so make sure to have an attentive belayer. A stick clip is helpful to hang all of the quick draws.
8 bolts. Lower-off anchors. (45 lateral feet).
*Ian Spencer Green and Darryl Roth*

**C.** **The Dark Arts** *5.13d* ****

An excellent route that starts with a V9 dyno to an ear (stick clip the first bolt), and continues with hard throws between good holds through the 5.13- section to a final V6 crux at the lip that guards the anchors. Classic powerful climbing up the 45 degree wall. One of the most fun and difficult routes in the canyon!
6 Fixed chain draws. Lower off anchors. (40 feet)
*Dan Durland '94*

D. **Open Project** *5.14d* ***
A V13 direct start to the Dark Arts, a futuristic line!

E. **Spew** *5.13a* ****
Great position! A crux boulder problem with a big cross-through to start takes you out the hanging arête, and then it's a question of whether or not you can hang on past the sloping crimpers, technical sequences, and building pump all the way to the chains.
5 bolts. Cold shut anchors. (40 feet)
*Darryl Roth '94*

F. **Surefire** *5.13d* ***
A recent addition to the wall, this crimpy route punches through three cruxes starting on *Spew*, doing a two bolt bouldery crux of its own, and finishing on *Rapture*. There are brief breaks between each crux, to give your crimping fingers a rest.
6 bolts. Cold shut anchors. (45 feet)
*Scott Hahn '08*

G. **Rapture** *5.13a* ***
A beautiful route that follows a technical V5 crux to a left-ward trending rail. Save some power for the dynamic lunge at the top which guards the anchors, which maybe height dependent. Great position and a good first 5.13a for you aspiring hard climbers!
5 bolts. Lower-off anchors. (45 feet)
*Dan Durland '94*

H. **Outré Salvo** *5.14a* ***
The newest and hardest route at the Spray Wall, follow easy climbing up the white arête to a very difficult V10 dyno using holds that all face the wrong way. Rest on the jugs, then jump into crimpy power-endurance and crack climbing all the way to the chains. Elevenmile's first 5.14, and currently the hardest route in the canyon!
6 bolts. Chain anchors. (50 feet)
*Ben Schmitt and Ian-Spencer Green '09*

I. **Pagan Wisdom** *5.12d* *
A decent route with interesting position. Start on the slab of *Only Entertainment*, and fire up left through a crimping crux and a hand jam to Outré Salvo's anchors. Many bouldery cruxes, with multiple places to rest in between.
6 bolts. Chain anchors. (50 feet)
*Ian-Spencer Green '94*

J. **Only Entertainment** *5.13b* ****
Absolutely classic technical power-endurance crimping. While the crux is the middle 1/3 of the climb, it is possible to fall off almost every move to the anchors. Get ready to pull on some small crimps! All natural and one of the best routes on the wall!
6 bolts. Cold shut anchors. (50 feet)
*Ian-Spencer Green and Mike Johnson '94*

**K. Mungamatic** *5.12a* *

Start on the beautiful black slab, and do balancy moves on great stone up to the crack in the corner. Follow the mungy crack past crimps and body jams to a stemming rest (or sit on the ledge) at 2/3 height. Do the final boulder problem past a big pinch to the anchors. Would be a much better 13a without the no hands ledge at 2/3 height.

6 bolts to cold shuts. (55 feet)

*Dan Durland '94*

*On the west facing panel on the right of the wall…*

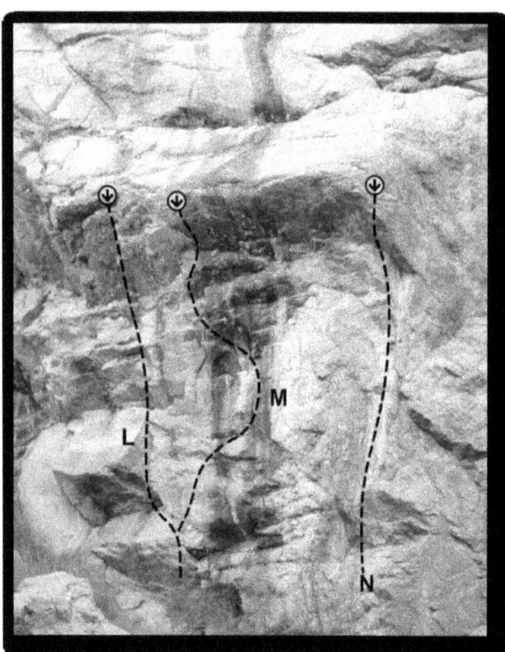


**L. Dad Speaks Parley** *5.10d* ***

Excellent moderate route with four distinct different cruxes separated by good rests. Powerful, pumpy, and technical. Recommend stick clipping the first bolt to protect the slab start.

5 bolts. Lower off anchors. (35 feet)

*Ed Schmitt and Ben Schmitt '08*

**M. Randy Speaks Farsi** *5.11a* ****

Best route of its grade almost anywhere, this pumpy climb starts at a slab and follows an ever steepening wave of black rock through many technical sequences to a final steep crux up top. Classic!

5 bolts. Lower off anchors. (35 feet)

*Bill Schmauser '93*

**N. Dan Speaks Darley** *5.11b* *

Follow the technical dihedral, stemming your way to a rest before the final crux lunge to a hidden hold up right over the lip.

5 bolts. Cold shut anchors. (35 feet)

*Dan Durland '94*

# Bigot Rock

*[Located immediately north of the road at 2.4 miles]*

Historically, this fine little crag has been the subject of some controversy. Parking below the cliff and shiny hangers on the rock attracted far too much attention, threatening access for climbing at Elevenmile all together. Recently, an effort has been made to camouflage hangers and keep a low profile. Please do not park directly under the cliff, but at the pullout 50 feet up and keep all belongings out of traffic.

Bigot Rock is comprised of two areas, the Arms Roof and Bigot Rock proper. Bigot Rock proper is the left facing dihedral ten feet from the road, and the Arms Race roof is 200 feet west and up the hill (recognized by its large overhanging characteristics). All five routes here are 5.12 and most are quality. The best time to climb here is during the weekdays, as you don't want to be fighting the traffic and crowded roads on the weekends.

**A.** **Will Power** *5.12a* **

Stem, lie-back, and finger lock your way up the main technical dihedral past the bulge and roof. Finish through the hand crack right to *Xenophobia's* anchors.
Medium-small wires, and cams to 2″.
Cold shut anchors. (35 feet)
*Bob D'Antonio '83*

**B.** **Xenophobia** *5.12d* **

An overlooked, but crimpy and continuous gem that takes the overhanging wall just right of *Will Power.* If it weren't for the long V5 move off the sloping under-cling at the third bolt (a long draw is useful), this would be a classic 5.12a.
6 bolts. Cold shut anchors. (35 feet)
*Darryl Roth '90*

C. **Just Do Me** *5.12c* ***

Take the striking arête past a low crux to finish just right of *Xenophobia.* Powerful pulling down low on sloping holds leads to excellent position up higher. Currently missing hangers.
5 bolts. Cold shut anchors. (35 feet)
*Darryl Roth '90*

D. **Arms Race** *5.12a* **

Incredibly sustained, pumpy finger tip climbing out and left in the obvious right facing dihedral in the roof. Gun for it, and you will be rewarded. Walk off at top. Pro to 3" with many finger sized cams and nuts. (30 feet)
*Bob D'Antonio '84*

E. **Open Project** *5.12d* *

This route has been top roped and bolted, but sports a red tag at the first cold shut and is missing hangers up high. It is also inhabited by swallows.
*Darryl Roth*

# The Tooth

*[Located immediately south of the road at 2.5 miles]*

This stunning formation always attracts they eye of keen climbers, but on closer inspection reveals poor rock quality and doesn't deliver as many routes as one might expect. However a few ok lines have been climbed on the feature, and are worth checing out if your looking for adventure.

**Approach:** Park at the bridge at 2.5 miles, in one of the pullouts (near the *Spray Wall* parking). Walk along the south side of the river on a fisherman's trail for 200 yards, and the wall will be visible on your left.

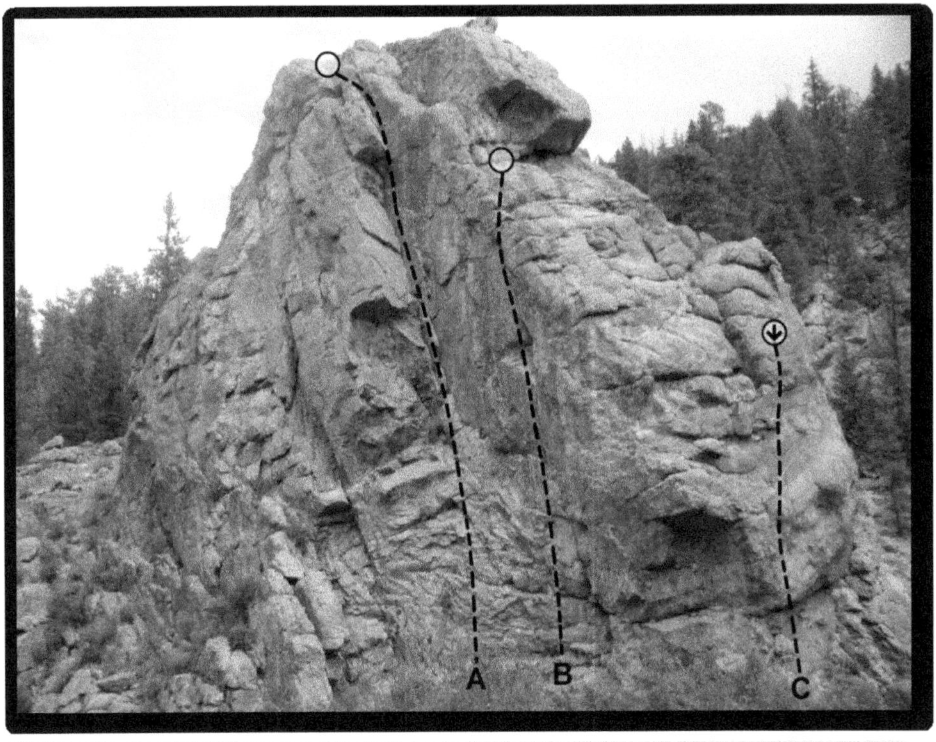

A. **Tooth Decay** *5.8 **

The cleanest line on the wall, take the low-angle, un-protectable slab up to join a large crack in the right facing dihedral. Build an anchor at the top of the cliff and scramble down the back side.
Nuts and Cams to 4". No Anchor. (120 feet)

B. **The Wound That Never Heals** *5.9 **

More like "the choss that never cleans up." Take the good looking splitter off the slab up the middle of the face to the ledge above, build a belay, and traverse around the roof (roped up!) to scramble down the backside.
Nuts and Cams to 4". No Anchor. (100 feet)
*Andy Brown and Lotus Steele '83*

C. **Novocain** *5.11d* * *

A little cleaner than the previous routes, but still a little loose. Climb the west face past bolts and multiple technical cruxes to an old rotten sling at the top of the cliff.
6 bolts. Sling anchor. 90 feet.

# *Elevenmile Dome*

## *[Located immediately north of the road at 2.7 miles]*

This incredible roadside cliff is often the most popular cliff in the canyon, and for good reason, as it hosts one of the highest concentrations of good beginner routes in Elevenmile! As one of the first domes in the canyon to receive development attention in the 1970's, Stewart Green, Brian Becker, Bob D'Antonio, Mike Johnson, and Russ Johnson are responsible for most of the routes here. Elevenmile Dome has gained popularity over the years because the rock is quality, the pitches are excellent, and the protection, for the most part, is good. Many of the routes here were originally established as bold run-out slab test pieces, with R/X death potential looming at every move. Fortunately, the ethic has changed in the past couple decades, as the re-bolting of these routes and the addition of belay anchors has inarguably made them much more enjoyable, safe, and quality outings which are loved by those who climb here! Many routes are multiple pitches, and are described as two pitch routes which require long links of the possible double short pitches on the slabs above the obvious first pitches. If at all in doubt, build a belay and break them up. I just find the longer pitch descriptions to be more enjoyable and efficient, and fortunately it's easy to rappel many of the routes due to the anchors scattered around the crag. **A 70 meter rope is very useful here, and would be an excellent idea to have as part of your Elevenmile climbing arsenal!**

**A.** **Kathy's Crack** *5.4*

Not shown in topo. On the very far left side of the cliff, this mossy crack takes the wide easy moss chute to large water pods at the top. Traverse left after 30 feet of bathtub climbing to build a belay and walk off the east gully.
Cams and nuts to 3". No Anchor. (80 feet)

**B.** **Stone Groove** *5.6* **

To the right of Kathy's crack lies a long, wide, right facing corner crack. Takes much larger gear and requires off-width and stemming techniques.
Medium and large cams to 5 inches. No anchor. (110 feet)

C. **The Overleaf** *5.8* ****

One of the most popular and quality moderates in this region! It's not uncommon to wait in line for this classic, but it is well worth it!

**Pitch 1:** (5.8): On the left side of the parking pullout, begin this climb up the large, obvious, right facing dihedral. Jam and lie-back up this nice feature, going right under a small roof, up the crack, to an option to either take a crux hand crack (5.8+) over the roof, or cut around the flake (5.9) and follow the lie-back to a cable anchor 30 feet up on top of the flake feature.
Full rack of cams and nuts to 4", lots of long slings. (120 feet)
**Pitch 2:** (5.6): Take the right facing dihedral feature crack up to the summit, and rather than building a belay, angle right to the cold shut anchors on the last pitch of *South Face Direct* and rappel down that route, or build a belay and walk-off left down the gully.
Medium cams and nuts to 2". Cold shut anchor. (80 feet)
Full rack of cams and nuts to 4", lots of long slings. (200 total feet)

D. **South Face Direct** *5.10c* ****

One of the better long routes on the cliff, and a good multi-pitch mixed route. Rappel via three rappels, to the various anchors or walk off left.
**Pitch 1** (5.10c): Starting on the furthest left line of bolts on the cliff, directly above the parking lot, this line climbs past two bolts through a technical off-balance crux to a long

section of easier run-out climbing above. Getting to the first bolt is heady, and having a stick clip would be a great idea.
6 bolts. Cold shut anchor. (95 feet)
**Pitch 2** (5.8 R): Fire directly up from the belay, getting gear where you can, up the vast slab with no move harder than 5.8 aiming for the left side of the roof that caps the dome. You will pass a set of cold shut anchors on your way, but it is better to run this out as one long pitch, and rap in three short rappels from the cold shut anchors at the start of *Ballabonkaphobia.*
Cams and nuts to 2". Cold shut anchor. (95 feet)
6 bolts. Cams and nuts to 3". (175 total feet)
*Russ Johnson and John Delong '82*

E. **Ballabonkaphobia** *5.11d* ***

Really fun final boulder problem pitch on the top of the dome! Approach by either hiking up the west side of the cliff via a steep gully and traversing across, or by *The Overleaf* and *Mike Johnson Route* final pitches. Belay from the cold shut anchors down and left, and angle up right to punch through the middle of the overhang to a devious crux topping out the lip. Well worth your while!
3 bolts. Coldshut anchors. (30 feet)

F. **Mike Johnson Route** *5.10b* ***

Run-out and old school, but very quality and a good route for those comfortable with 5.10. This pitch climbs a long section of 5.8 climbing to a perplexing sloper crux at the bulge. Continue up to share belay at anchors over the lip with *Face Value.* A second pitch has been done, which is not very good, taking the run-out 5.8 face above to build an anchor below the roof, and takes nuts and cams to 3 inches.
6 bolts. Chain anchors. (80 feet)
*Mike Johnson*

G. **Face value** *5.8* ****

Starting off the small ledge, 20 feet off the ground, there are two routes which have very close starting points. Face value takes the left line directly off the ledge through a brief technical crux to follow beautiful crystallized features up the gorgeous wall. Well protected, popular, and definitely lives up to the hype.
8 bolts. Chain anchors. (90 feet)
*Bob D'Antonio*

H. **Miss Wyoming** *5.9* ****

On the right side of the ledge, angle up and right through a sustained technical crux, to easier climbing past bullet rock on interesting features. Another popular classic that is just as good and a bit harder than its neighbor *Face Value.*
8 bolts. Chain anchor. ( 90 feet)
*Bob D'Antonio*

I. **Cheryl's Peril** *5.9* ***

Popular for how run-out and sporty it is. Start 20 feet right of *Miss Wyoming,* and take the long varied slab past flakes and crystals to anchors over the lip. The run-outs are relatively safe, and supplemented by good gear in the flakes. **Requires a 70m rope to rappel!**

4 bolts, cams and nuts to 3". Chain anchor (95 feet)

*Brian Becker '78*

*J.* **Repulsion Convulsion** *5.10c*

An abandoned project accidently FA'd by Chris during a rainstorm. 30 feet right of *Cheryl's Peril* this pile takes the line over the short vertical face past a new camouflaged brown bolt to one of the most run-out and poorly bolted piles in Elevenmile. Pull the death roof to shared anchors with *The Great Unknown.* **Requires a 70m rope to rappel!**

8 bolts. Chain anchor. (110 feet)

*Chris Barlow '10*

**K.** **The Great Unknown** *5.10a* **

Listed as "Unknown 5.9" for years, this route starts left of *Counter Strike* and follows long sport slab edges up and left to a roof. Although poorly bolted, this route seems to retain popularity. **Requires a 70m rope to rappel!**
7 bolts. Chain anchor. (120 feet)

**L.** **Counter Strike** *5.5* ***

A popular easy lead that follows a stitched slab up the middle of the face 30 feet left of the *Moby Grape* dihedral, and 30 feet right of *The Great Unknown* to anchors below the small roof. Good, easy climbing with a high crux.
9 bolts. Chain anchor. (90 feet)
*Bill Schmausser*

**M.** **Phantom Pinnacle** *5.7 R* **

A varied, traditional route that is worth doing if you're looking for an adventure and want to weave all over Elevenmile Dome.
**Pitch 1**(5.7): *Variation 1*: Starting 30 feet left of the Moby Grape Dihedral, there is an obvious left trending arch, which marks the start of the climb. Under-cling the arch up and left as long as possible, then fire up the easy un-protectable slab for 30 feet aiming for the right side of the short roof 15 feet right of Counter Strikes anchors. Pull the small crux roof and cut up left to belay above the cave arch near a bush in a small alcove.
*Variation 2:* Start ten feet right of the left angling arch, and climb up the poorly protectable slab for 50 feet aiming for the right side of the roof, and join the previous variation to pull the roof and build the same belay. Pull the small crux roof and cut up left to belay above the cave arch near a bush in a small alcove.
Cams and nuts to 2 inches. No anchor. (125 feet)
**Pitch 2:** (5.6): Follow a hand crack up and left aiming for the right side of another small roof, and jam the right side of the roof and angle back up right to join another hand crack that leads straight up to the large roof past an old piton. Build a belay here, and then traverse (roping up would be a good idea!) left underneath the large roof to walk off the gully on the left side of the cliff. Cams and nuts to 3" . No anchor. (160 feet)
Cams and nuts to 3". (285 total feet)

**N.** **More Tea Vicar?** *5.7* **

A recent mixed addition to the dome, this route is a little better quality than *Phantom Pinnacle*, and much more direct.
**Pitch 1**(5.7): Start as you would for variation 2 of *Phantom* on the slab just left of *Moby*, and take the relatively un-protectable face up and left to a hanging right facing dihedral with a water pod above. Once at the dihedral, pull the lip, and climb through the pod past bolts to a bolted anchor.
5 bolts, small to medium nuts and cams to 2" . Chain anchor. (125 feet)
**Pitch 2** (5.6): Launch off the belay and join the left trending cracks and seams which angle up toward the roof and belay from the second pitch of *Phantom.* There is no distinct line here, but any way you go is no harder than 5.6 and ends at the same place.

Traverse left under the roof (roping up is a good idea!) to walk off the gullies left of the cliff. Cams and nuts to 3"  No anchor. (125 feet)
Cams and nuts to 3 inches, and 5 quick draws. (250 total feet)
*Stewart Green, Brian Shelton, Dennis Jump '09*

**O.** **Moby Grape** *5.7* **

Although this route is a little loose, people still enjoy it and don't be surprised to wait in line. This route is a decent climb to learn to place gear on, although others in the canyon offer much better alternatives. It is preferable to climb the first pitch and rappel. **Note that a 70 meter rope is required to reach the ground!**

**Pitch 1:** (5.7) In the obvious right racing dihedral stem and finger jam for 120 feet past marginal rock, good nut placements, and a bulge crux below the anchors under the roof system.
Cams and a wide range of nuts to 2". Chain anchor. (120 feet)

**Pitch 2:** *Variation 1:* (5.10a) Punch through the juggy hand crack above the anchors, and cut back left through a small run-out to join incipient cracks which angle up left to a bolted belay below the roof. Annoying rope drag, and not that great of a pitch.
*Variation 2: (5.6)* Step left under the roof and angle up through incipient cracks to a bolted belay below the roof. Traverse left to walk off (Rope up!) the left side of the dome, or rap down to *Cheryl's Peril* anchors using double 60m ropes, and then to the ground.
Cams and a wide range of nuts to 2". (220 total feet)
*Larry Schubarth and Greg Stevens '78*

P. **Original Sin** *5.9* ***

Originally done with run-out gear and a few bolts, this route is now a fully equipped sport climb. Just to the right of *Moby Grape,* climb the sustained slab past multiple cruxes and bolts that are hard to see from the ground, to end at anchors shared with *Moby Grape.* **Note you need a 70m rope to comfortably lower!**
8 bolts. Chain anchor. (110 feet)
*Stewart Green and Martha Morris '96*

Q. **Jet Setter** *5.8 R/X*

A contrived, wandering route that needs updating due to multiple places to kill yourself. Decent rock and cool moves, but other routes on this wall are far better!
**Pitch 1:** (5.7 R/X) Between the two bolted lines of *Original Sin* and *Happy Trails* this line takes the 40 foot unprotected death slab up and right to climb through the middle of a small, left facing, overhanging roof arch. Cross *Happy Trails,* clip one of its bolts, and angle up right to build a belay under the right side of the roof.
Full rack of cams and nuts to 3". No anchor. (130 feet)
**Pitch 2:** (5.6): Step right around the roof from the belay, and angle up right through run-out, easy ground aiming for a juggy break in the roof system. Build a belay below the roof at the horizontal break.
Full rack of cams and nuts to 3". No anchor. (100 feet)
**Pitch 3:** (5.8): Climb juggy flakes over the small roof, through a heady crux, and solo up easy ground to build a belay or find a tree at the summit.
Full rack of cams and nuts to 3". No anchor. (100 feet)
Full rack of cams and nuts to 3". (330 total feet)
*Stewart Green, Johnny Myers, and Ed Russel '79*

R. **Happy Trails** *5.6* **

An old traditional pitch that was re-bolted (on lead) to yield a decent beginner route, although it will feel quite run-out for the 5.6 leader and hard for the grade. This is the second bolted route right of the *Moby* dihedral, and takes the slab to a crux up the small pointed nose feature to a thin crux above. **You need a 70m rope to lower!**
6 bolts. Cold shut anchor. (110 feet)
*Stewart Green '79 and Mark Vanhorn '94*

S. **EZ Street** *5.9 ***

Another easier pitch that usually experiences less traffic than those on the left side of the dome.

**Pitch 1:** (5.5) Starting just left of the pine tree, take the easy, well protected slab past 3 bolts and easy moves to an anchor below the roof. A good lead that may be supplemented with small nuts and cams.

3 bolts, nuts and cams to 2". Rappel Anchor. (90 feet)

**Pitch 2:** (5.9) Angle up right past a bolt to punch through the crux bolt protected roof, and angle back up and left through water pods to a bolted anchor. You may do a terrible third and fourth pitch (Shared with *Jet Setter)* but it's not worth it as most people just do the first two pitches.

4 bolts. Chain anchor. (40 feet)

*Stewart Green, John Meyers, and Ed Russel '79*

# Wildflower Gulch

*[Located immediately north of the road at 3.4 miles]*

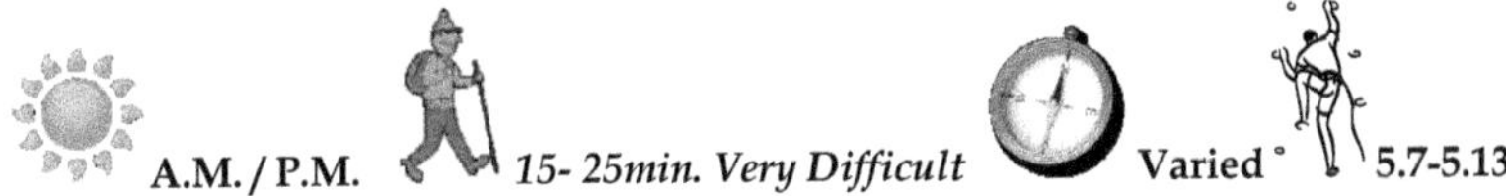


The Wildflower Gulch complex is one of the newest crags in Elevenmile, and has an enourmous potential for development for those willing to do the approach. Srambling around the gully is akin to the Battan Death March, battling loose rocks, a difficult scree field, thorn bushes, and poor footing. The first two walls to be developed in the canyon were Tinaja Dome and the Wildflower Wall, both by Stewart Green and Brian Shelton in 2007. In 2010 Ben Schmitt and Chris Barlow explored the "Nose" feature, a proud jutting pice of rock out of the gulche's south side to add a small piece to this massive area.

**Approach:** Park at the pullout before the bridge at 3.4 miles and head up the side canyon on the right side of the road. Tinaja Dome is visible on the north side of the canyon from the parking, and is a difficult 10 or 15 minute approach to reach its base. The nose is hidden from view until you reach Tinaja, and is directly across from that crag. The Wildflower Wall is reached by skirting the base of Tinaja and heading up the gully until the canyon opens up to a beautiful wide meadow. Wildflower Dome is on the right side of the meadow, and is reached after a 20 -25 minute hike.

## Tinaja Dome

A dome with a lot more devlopment potential for good moderates. A few in progress routes at the time of writing, but one worth doing as a warmup for the other routes in the area.

A. **Ribs** *5.8 **

Above two large boulders on the north side of the creek, this route takes the large narrow bulge of stone just right of a large off-width. Cruxy, sustained climbing leads to easier climbing above to a ledge. NO TOPO.
3 bolts. Single bolt anchor. (50 feet)
*Stewart Green and Brian Shelton '07*

# The Nose

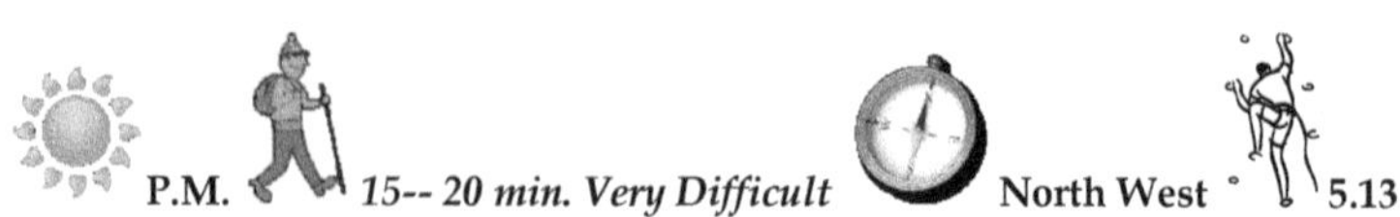


A beautiful feature with potential for harder routes, The Nose hosts one worthwhile climb for those who can climb the grade and desire a little solitude or refuge from the heat.

**A.** **Archaeopteryx** *5.13c* **

A quality bouldery route up the west side of the nose feature. Start right and cut up left traversing a rail to a brutal dynamic crux throw to a sloping ledge that has been the stopping point of many shorter climbers. Finish up through technical V3 climbing to anchors.

5 bolts. Cold shut anchors. (40 feet)

*Ben Schmitt, Chris Barlow, and Rivet Daigre '10*

Logan Davis on *Intercontinental* (5.10c) at Heaven's Gate

# Arch Rock

*[Located uphill on the south side of the road at 3.7 miles]*

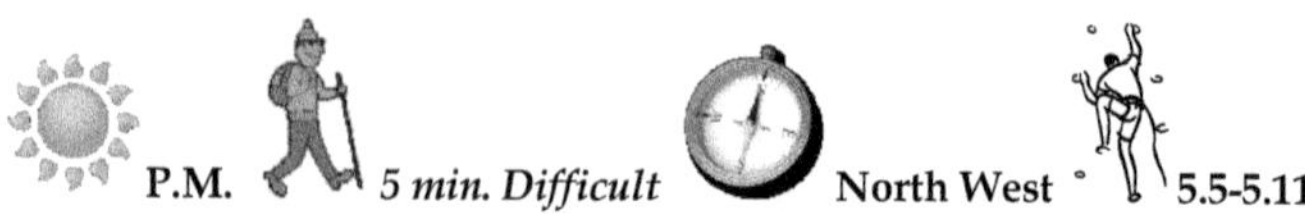


Renowned for its quality moderates, Arch Rock is a great place to take first time climbers on stunning multi pitch adventures. Due to its northwest facing aspect, this is an excellent summer crag, and often is the place to meet friendly climbers and fellow outdoorsmen to share an afternoon in a superb setting overlooking the South Platte River. The crag had to have seen its first ascent in the 1960's, during training for the various clubs. However Brian Becker and Stewart Green added many of the crag's earlier routes, followed by the additions of Bill Schmausser to create one of the canyon's most popular cliffs.

**A.** **Smiley Face** *5.7* **

On the far left side of the cliff, away from the other routes, climb a low-angle section up to a small ledge, then take varied technical climbing to anchors up and right of the right facing flake. A well protected, good warm up!
4 bolts. Ring anchors. (75 feet)
*Stewart Green and Martha Morris '06*

**B.** **The Staircase** *5.5* ****

Phenomenally beautiful, and utterly classic; this may be one of the best 5.5 pitches in Colorado! Taking the proud dihedral line up the "upside down staircase," this route is certainly a must do for any moderate climber.
**Pitch 1** (5.4): Begin atop a small ledge and follow the slabby crack, past jugs, stems, and perfect jams up the middle of the face. The crux is at the very beginning, but technical moves on the slab guard the belay ledge at the break in the face.
Nuts and cams to a #3 Camalot, no anchor. (60 feet)
**Pitch 2** (5.5): From the belay ledge, stem your way up the short, beautiful crux dihedral to water pods over the lip. Climb through the easy dihedral, to a bulge with a crack in it or a ledge up and left. The original route cuts up and left, the skirts back right to the top, while the variation (5.8) takes the overhanging hand crack over the lip to the belay.
Nuts and cams to a #4 Camalot, no anchor (55 feet)
Bring a full rack of nuts and cams to 4". (115 feet)

Variation
C
B
J
K
F
A
B
D
E
G
H
I

C. **Haircase** *5.11b R* *

A variation to the *Staircase*, begin up its first pitch to build a belay at the obvious belay ledge, from here cut directly up left through the overlapped roofs, placing marginal gear, past a brief bolt protected crux, then take one more bolt up and right to gain a ledge that rejoins the *Staircase* at its belay. Would be much more popular with an update.
2 bolts, nuts and cams to 2.5". No anchor. (60 feet)
*Andy Brown*

D. **Waiting on a Resolution** *5.9+ R* *

Just to the right of *Staircase,* take the run-out crux panel (a recommended stick clip!) past the small bulge to long, easy climbing above. Originally done as a variation on the *Staircase* without the bolts. Definitely has the feel of the old South Platte sport ethic, and subsequently has been the scene of many broken ankles! **Use a 70m rope for rappel!**
7 bolts. Chain Anchor. (120 feet)
*Brian Becker '76*

E. **Kansas Honey** *5.9* **

Re-bolted in the '80s, this route has now become quite popular. Begin just right of the small tree, taking slightly run-out crux moves past two bolts to a long, easy moderate section all the way to the anchors. A seldom done second pitch takes the crack through the small roof, and finishes up easier climbing over a long 60m pitch to belay at the top of the cliff using cams and nuts to 3".
8 bolts. Chain anchor. (115 feet)
*Leonard Coyne and Ed Russell '80*

F. **Waiting on the Staircase** *5.7* ***

The best of the three sport pitches on this panel, take easy low-angle climbing past well protected crux moves to sustained edging and multiple rest up the vast slab. A good one to do with a large group!
6 bolts. Chain anchor. (90 feet)

G. **Hollow Flake** *5.6* ***

This superb, moderate traditional pitch is a great place to teach new leaders to place gear. Take either the right trending ramp crack (5.5), or the slightly more difficult direct off-width (5.6), and lie-back and stem up a nice corner to anchors over the lip. Superb!
Nuts and cams to 4". Chain anchor (65 feet)

H. **Zamboni Man** *5.10d* ***

The beautiful arête in the middle of the panel. Climb past some interesting technical moves to a low crux at the second bolt, then fire up the beautiful arête to a high and ultra thin crux. Very nice position to a ledge over the lip!
6 bolts. Chain anchor. (60 feet)
*Bill Schmausser '96*

I. **Sprout Route** *5.11R/X*

15 feet right of *Zamboni*, take the thin, un-protectable seams up and left past two bolts (and a lot of places to fall) over slightly easier ground to shared anchors with *Zamboni* and *Hollow Flake*. There is a good reason no one does this. The second pitch has been annexed into *Persistence.*
Nuts and cams to 1.5". Chain anchor (65 feet)
*Leonard Coyne '82*

*The next two routes are variation second pitches above the belay ledge with the small tree…*

J. **Persistence** *5.9* ***

Exposed, beautiful climbing off the belay ledge above *Zamboni* (which is the best start for this route). Take the thin slab up and left to a roof which can be protected by a small cam, then pull the crux roof edge up nice moves to anchors. Most people rappel from here; however, there is a small third pitch which takes a single bolt and gear to 3" up a crack to the summit. **You must use a 70m rope for rappel!**
10 bolts, cams to 1". Chain anchor. (100 feet)
*Bill Schmausser '97*

K. **Pride of Sweden** *5.10b* ****

The best sport pitch on the cliff. Traverse 15 feet right of the anchors to a small pine tree on the ledge. Belay here, and climb up the bullet slab, edging up to a high-step crux over the roof. Continue up sustained and superb climbing which angles back left to share anchors with *Persistence.* **You must use a 70m rope for rappel!**
9 bolts. Chain anchor. (100 feet)
*Bill Schmausser '97*

*Up a small boulder filled gully 25 feet right of Sprout Route….*

L. **Death by Drowning** *5.10d R* **

A quality, but intimidating route over beautiful features. This route was hand drilled by the FA party during a rainstorm, hence the name!
**Pitch 1:** (5.5) Take the mossy, dirty cracks up and left through easy climbing to build a belay at the break on the right end of the ledge with the pine tree.
Cams and nuts to 3". No anchor. (40 feet)
**Pitch 2:** (5.10d R) Angle up and right through superb sustained climbing past multiple bolts to a death run-out (which may be protected by some marginal TCU cams) to an anchor distinctly obscure and away from the rest of the climbing. This is the best pitch,

and can also be accessed by climbing left from the first pitch of *Captain Fist*. A wandering vague third pitch cuts through the roofs above the anchors, however it's not worth doing.
4 bolts. Chain anchor. (70 feet)
**You must use a 70m rope for rappel!**
9 bolts. Chain anchor. (100 feet)
*Stewart Green '97*

**M.** **Captain Fist** *5.8 R* ***

A fun little route up the dihedral crack on the left side of the large block perched against the cliff on the right side of the crag. Start by making tricky 5.7 moves up the unprotected slab to gain the crack and place your first large piece. Climbing eases off significantly after this, taking nice jams and cool stemming to the top of the boulder.
Medium and large cams to 4". Cable Anchor (45 feet)
*Brian Teale and Dan Morrison '74*

**N.** **In Two Deep** *5.10d* **

On the right side of the cave, 5 feet right of *Captain Fist* climb the obvious large roof crack out the belly of the cave to a crux pulling around the lip, angle up left to join the anchors of *Captain Fist*. Cool roof off-width!
Large cams and Big Bro's to 8". Cable Anchor (45 feet)

*To the right, 15 feet around the corner on the main face of the pillar…*

**O.** **Arch Rock Direct** *5.7 ***

A combination of three decent pitches, this popular route is most commonly done to the top of the pinnacle after doing one of *The Meanie Cracks* and finishing (inevitably) on *Middle Dihedral.*

**Pitch 1:** (5.7) Take any of the three obvious 15 foot splitter cracks (named the *Meanie Cracks)* on the main panel, ending at a ledge. The middle crack is the best, but all three offer nice 5.7 hand-jamming practice. Belay at the ledge or link the pitch and continue up the face (called *Middle Dihedral)* to hidden anchors on top of the pinnacle.
Nuts and Cams to 3". Rappel Anchor (60 feet)

**Pitch 2:** (5.7) Step right off the pinnacle and angle up past two bolts (passing bolted anchors on your right after 30 feet) to run-out, but much easier terrain over bathtubs. Aim for the break in the roof, and pull it (5.6) to continue up low-angle terrain and belay at the summit.
Nuts and Cams to 3". No Anchor (70 feet)
*Brian Becker '75*

*Just right of the pillar….*

**P.** **Zendance** *5.7 R/X ***

A popular, but extremely dangerous pitch that has been the sight of many broken ankles and near deaths. Bolted on rappel as a sport climb, but you definitely want to bring extra pro and make sure you are a competent 5.10 leader before attempting this lead.

**Pitch 1:** (5.7R/X) Stick clip the first bolt, and fire past the crux over the steep panel and angle up and left along a small dike past harrowing run-outs to clip two more bolts over easier terrain to the anchors.

**You must use a 70m rope to lower!**

4 bolts, Nuts and Cams to 2". Rappel Anchor (100 feet)

**Pitch 2:** (5.7) Run-out but much easier terrain over bathtubs. Aim for the break in the roof, and pull it (5.6) to continue up low-angle terrain and belay at the summit.
Nuts and Cams to 3". No Anchor (50 feet)
*Stewart Green and Ian Green '94*

**Q.** **Obscura Direct** *5.7 X **

Once a "classic," this vegetated and horrendously run-out route is now usually avoided since the addition of newer, better climbs on the wall. Don't make this your first choice if you lead below 5.10.

**Pitch 1:** (5.5) Begin atop a small boulder ledge, 30 feet down and right of the tower, and climb up the 5.5 crack. Cut right across a traverse for 20 feet, and build an anchor directly below the right facing dihedral.
Nuts and Cams to 3". No Anchor (80 feet)

**Pitch 2:** (5.7 X) climb up the right facing dihedral for 30 feet, then angle up left over continuously easy climbing for 70 feet via a terrifying, death inviting, run-out to the

break in the arch. Plug in gear, stop from shaking, and pull the easier roof and climb the groove to belay at the summit.
Nuts and Cams to 3". No Anchor. (120 feet)
*Brian Becker '75*

R. **Black Jack** *5.8* ***

A.K.A. Arch Rock Route. This is a popular pitch on the right side of the dome.

**Pitch 1:** (5.5) Take the right angling crack, past a little vegetation, to a nice face crack which leads straight up to a comfy belay ledge. A handful of variations, from 5.7-5.9, can be done as substitutes, but all lead to the same place.
Nuts and Cams to 3". No anchor (65 feet)

**Pitch 2:** (5.7 X) A long pitch following the crack above the belay which leads to a large off-width at the top of the dome. Difficult to protect, but easy climbing through the off-width climbs up through a "hole" and 5.6 terrain to the summit. Walk off right, down the hill.
Nuts and Cams to 3". No Anchor (140 feet)
*Brian Becker '75*

# Turret Dome

*[Located across the river on the north side of the road at 4.1 miles]*

Unrivaled in height by any crag in Elevenmile, Turret Dome's massive figure dominates the banks of the South Platte with authoritative presence. Its inviting slabs beckon those keen to climb on stellar rock for multiple pitches, as the sprawling slabs rise from river to summit for over 450 feet. While the crag's southern slabs have occupied guides and early climbers since the 70's, the newer western faces have received much deserved attention through their development at the beginning of the new millennium. Bill Schmausser, Bob D'Antonio, and Stewart Green are the main activists responsible for the fine new routes that have gone in, and it is definitely worth any climber's time to give this area a visit for the day.

*Routes listed from right to left (from where the trail meets the river to the climbs on the west face high on the hillside)…*

**A.** ***Vulture*** 5.10c **

Where the trail meets the cliff, take the class 3 steep gully between Turret Dome and the large, west facing ridge cliff band (called Eagle Ridge). Halfway up the gully (on your right) there is a mixed line which takes a large slab split by horizontal seams. Rappel from an anchor by a detached block at the top of the route.

3 bolts, Nuts and Cams to 3". Quick-link anchor. (90 feet)

*Stewart Green*

*Routes listed from right to left (from where the trail meets the river to the climbs on the west face high on the hillside)…*

**B.** ***Sunshine Face*** 5.3 ***

On the sprawling South face of Turret Dome, there is a huge 500 foot tall by 100 foot wide slab. Speckled with bathtubs, cracks, and ledges, any number of routes and variations can be taken up this face ranging from 5.0 to 5.3. Excellent, long, easy pitches (usually about 4 or 5), get you to the summit where you can walk off the top right side of the dome. It is likely you will see slings or remnants of old anchors, but you really can't go wrong anywhere on the slab as many undocumented variations have been done.

Cams and nuts to 4". No Anchors. (500 feet)

C. **_Upper Lip_** _5.7 **_

A good finish to any of the long easy routes up the _Sunshine Slab_. At the top of the dome there is a bulge that caps the slabs. This route takes the prominent summit crack over the upper lip, via five moves of 5.7 hand-jamming to finish up and right round the corner to build a belay.

Cams to 5″. No Anchor. (60 feet from belay ledge below crack)

D. **_Fishhook_** _5.5 *_

Hiking up the trail, this is the obvious right arching, low-angle, under-cling crack that angles under a large face. Funky protection, loose rock, and some contrived belaying comprise this ok route. Finish up right around the corner and belay off the trees up left off the top of the wall, or join any of the sunshine routes to the top of the cliff.

Cams to 4″. No Anchor. (70 feet)

E. **_The Worm_** _5.8_

30 feet to the left of _Fishhook_ take the left facing corner up stems and face climbing to trees over the lip. Not recommended.

Nuts and Cams to 4″. Tree anchor. (80 feet)

F. *Jaws 5.6* **

Another moderate climb, worth doing for the awesome under-clings on the lower pitches and the interesting bathtubs on the upper ones.

**Pitch 1:** (5.4) Begin right of a pine tree, taking a wide, right facing dihedral up and left over easy climbing for 60 feet and cut up and right over 5.3 climbing to belay at a tree. Nuts and cams to 6″. (90 feet)

**Pitch 2:** (5.6): Take the long left facing, gradually steepening dihedral via endless under-clinging up left to the break in the roof on the left side of the arch. **Use a 70m rope** or break this up into two smaller pitches. Build a belay below the small roof. Cams to 6″. No Anchor. (120 feet)

**Pitch 3:** (5.5) Exit left out of the arch over a small roof, then angle back right through a long, run-out slab over huge bathtubs to build a belay under the large roof. Bring lots of slings to mitigate rope drag.
Cams and nuts to 4″. (120 feet)

**Pitch 4:** (5.5-5.7) Take either the low-angle, left splitter crack through the small roof 30 feet left off the belay (5.5) for 70 feet up incipient cracks to the summit, or climb the *Upper Lip* finish. Alternatively, climb the 4th class walk off out right to join the gully which leads to the bottom of the crag. The most popular is *Upper Lip.*
Nuts and cams to 6″. (450 total feet)

G. **Knup** *5.7* ***X***

Take the wide, shallow, pink dihedral 30 feet left of the start of *Jaws* and angle up the un-protectable slab to join *Jaws* 2/3 of the way up. It's a good thing this style has died out (maybe worth doing if it had bolts) because as of now it's a death route. Nuts and Cams to 6″. No Anchor. (70 feet from belay ledge below crack)
*Larry Schubarth and Jen Walkup '77*

H. **Schooldaze** *5.6 ****

The most popular traditional route on the dome, and understandably, as the varied climbing up awesome features, cool exposure, and ease of access, makes this a brilliant endeavor.

**Pitch 1:** (5.6): Start up the gully that comprises the left side of the obvious 250 foot arch, which graces the southwest side of Turret Dome. This incredibly long pitch takes the right facing, gradually steepening dihedral up to the break in the roof on the left side of the arch. **Use a 70m rope** or break this up into two smaller pitches. Build a belay below the small roof.
Cams to 6″. No Anchor. (200 feet)

**Pitch 2:** (5.5) Exit left out of the arch over a small roof, then angle back right through a long, run-out slab over huge bathtubs, to build a belay under the large roof. Bring lots of slings to mitigate rope drag.

**Pitch 3:** (5.5-5.7) Take either the low-angle, left splitter crack through the small roof 30 feet left off the belay (5.5) for 70 feet up incipient cracks to the summit, or climb the *Upper Lip* finish. Alternatively, climb the 4th class walk off out right to join the gully which leads to the bottom of the crag. The most popular is *Upper Lip.*
Nuts and cams to 6″. No anchor. (450 total feet)

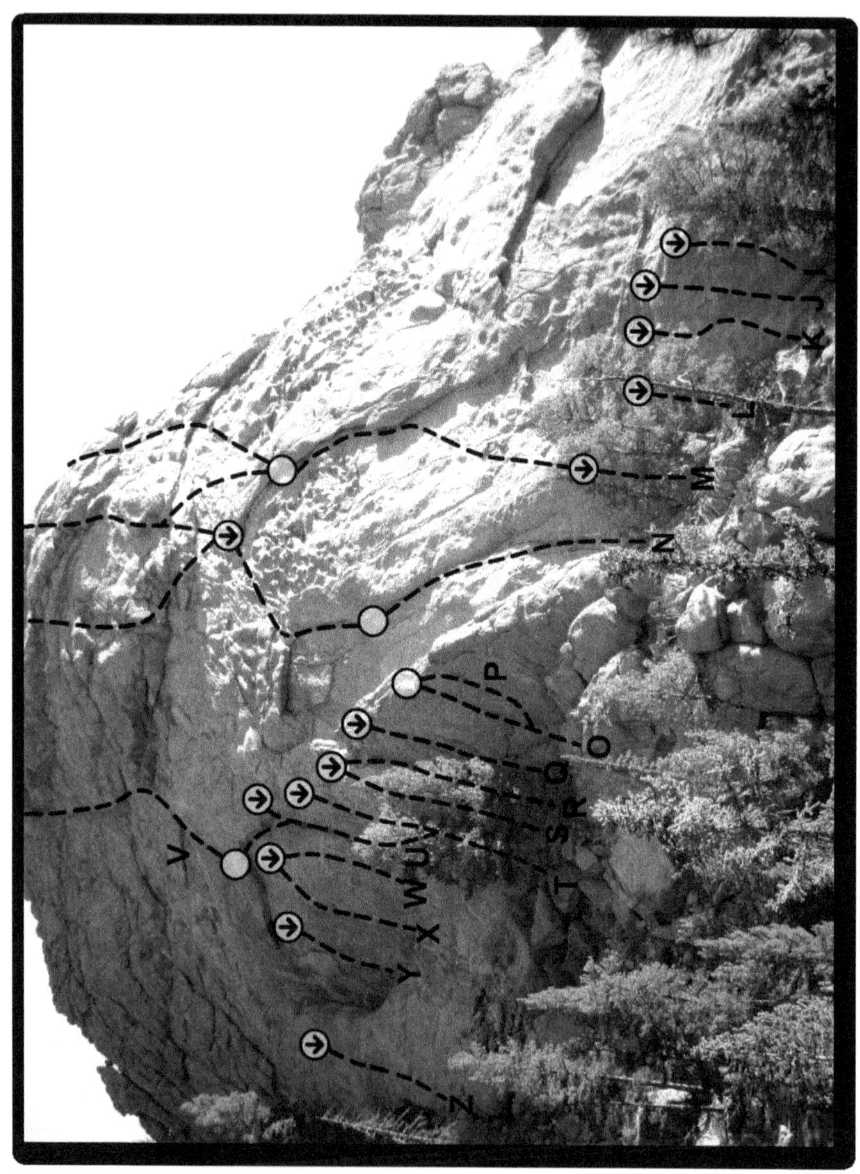
I
J
K
L
M
N
O
P
Q
R
S
T
U
V
W
X
Y
Z
V

*100 feet uphill from Schooldaze to the left of the large pine tree, lies a moderate size alcove which hosts some quality sport routes, the first being…*

I. **Sloppy Shoes** *5.10a ****

Start up the right side of the face to plug a 3″ cam in the large under-cling flake. Punch up to a shallow crux groove, and stem and smear up and left to join the 4th bolt of *Car Stud* to finish on that route. Good technical climbing.
5 bolts, 3″ cam. Quick link anchors. (65 feet)
*Stewart Green and Dennis Jump '04*

J. **Car Stud** *5.9 ***

8 feet to the left of *Sloppy*, climb past a low bolt and run-out, but easy climbing (which can be supplemented with a 3″ cam) to a thin smearing crux at the third bolt. Then it's easy climbing up over a bulge to anchors. There is an orphan bolt up and left between this route and *The Mexicanist*.
5 bolts, 3″ cam. Quick link anchors. (60 feet)
*Bill Schmausser and Britt Anderson '00*

K. **The Mexicanist** *5.10a ***

On the left side of the small alcove, stem your way up the small wall behind the start of the route, then climb well protected balancy moves up and right, then back left to a perplexing side-pull crux at the 4th bolt to much easier moves to the anchors.
6 bolts. Quick link anchors. (60 feet)
*Bill Schmausser and Britt Anderson '00*

*A small 15 foot scramble up the gully yields…*

L. **Capitalist Revenge** *5.9 ***

Clip a bolt close off the ground, then fire up right over cool jugs, which lead to easier technical climbing to the anchors in a bathtub feature over the lip.
5 bolts. Quick link anchors. (40 feet)
*Bill Schmausser and Britt Anderson '00*

M.  **Velvet Habel** *5.7 ***

**Pitch 1:** (5.7) 20 feet up and left of *Capitalist*, clip a bolt close off the ground, then climb up and right past technical, slightly mossy climbing to easier rock after the third bolt, then up and right to anchors in the bathtub.
5 bolts. Quick link anchors. (50 feet)
**Pitch 2:** (5.7) Also known as *Turret Direct* take slightly run-out climbing up and right to join the crack in the left facing corner flake. Continue up the corner all the way up to build an anchor below the blocky 20 foot wide roof. This makes for a long pitch which might require some long slings for rope drag, and **also might need a 70m rope**!
Cams and nuts to 3″. No anchor. (120 feet)

**Pitch 3:** (5.5-5.9) A short pitch, either go directly up through the more difficult roof system, or cut right past a pin and then go straight up through multiple flakes to the summit. Any way you go will be fine, but take lots of long runners to minimize rope drag. The original route goes right…
Cams and nuts to 3". No anchor. (50 feet)
*Bill Schmausser and Britt Anderson '01*

*30 feet uphill from the sport routes in a small alcove with two large pine trees lies….*

**N.** **Guides Route** *5.6 ***

This climb has been popular for a long time, although mainly as an easy climb to get clients up the vast expanse of Turret Dome. The start of the route is obvious; however, after the second pitch there are many variations depending on whether you go direct (5.9) or right (5.6). Bring lots of runners for this route.
**Pitch 1:** (5.6): Starting in the gully 30 feet up left from *Velvet Habel,* this route begins up an obvious crack system behind two pine trees which are identified by three cracks which angle up and converge over the lip. Begin up the rightmost of these three cracks, making easy moves for a ways over well protected ground to a crux at a fixed ring. Pull this move, then angle up and left to build an anchor at a belay ledge right below a roof.
Cams and nuts to 4". No Anchor. (90 feet)
**Pitch 2:** (5.5) Take the left facing, shallow dihedral directly up to the right side of the roof. Then follow the run-out easy bathtubs up and right to find a three pin anchor on top of an overhang of the major left facing dihedral.
Cams and nuts to 4". Three pin anchor. (45 feet)
**Pitch 3:** (5.5-5.9) Another short pitch, either go directly up through the more difficult roof system, or cut right past a pin and then go straight up through multiple flakes to the summit. Any way you go will be fine, but take lots of long runners to minimize rope drag. The original route goes right…
Cams and nuts to 4". No Anchor. (45 feet)
Cams and nuts to 4". (200 total feet)

*Heading up hill from the guides route alcove, angle left between a large fallen tree and some boulders, cut immediatly right and surmount a small pointed boulder, then head up through a tight squeeze into a long, 20 foot tunnel which deposits you directly below….*

**O.** **Aid Route** *5.10a ***

On the far right side of the panel, climb the finger tip splitter through a micro roof up through sustained ground and deteriorating rock to the lip. The anchor is sketchy, so it's best to build a belay and traverse left to rappel off of *Anya's* bolts.
Cams and nuts to 1.5". Sling anchor. (50 feet)
*Pete Williams and Pete Gallagher '79*

**P.** **Test Pattern** *5.10c R **

Start as for *Aid Route* but break right through a dangerous crux after 10 feet to join another finger crack and shallow dihedral of its own. Belay as for *Aid Route.*
Cams and nuts to 1.5". Sling anchor. (50 feet)

Q. **Anya Direct** *5.11a* *

Just right of *Canine,* take the slabby tombstone feature up to an obvious jug crystal protruding out of a roof. Clip a hard to reach bolt, then crux it up the deteriorating face past two sketchy cam placements to pull the roof to anchors over the lip.

4 bolts, .5 cam, 2" cam. Quick link anchor. (65 feet)

*Bill Schmausser*

*Just to the left of Anya on a separate panel of its own…*

R. **Canine Rescue** *5.10a* ****

Absolutely stellar! This well protected and long route would be an excellent choice for someone breaking into leading 5.10. Begin on the far right side of the panel, 10 feet right of *White Stress* and take the left angling, low-angle dihedral up and over a roof to the slab above where a high technical crux guards the anchors.

9 bolts. Quick link anchors. (90 feet)

*Bill Schmausser*

S. **White Stress** *5.12a R/X* ***

This '80s classic is a must do top rope until it can be updated. Marked by the rusty quarter inch button head at the start, take this beautiful hard slab past two bolts to a brief rest, then up left past two more bolts to a crux to join the micro seam to *Canine Rescue's* anchors. With no pro, very poorly and dangerously placed bolts, and the death run-out to the top, you'd have to be insane to lead this…

4 bolts, micro wires. Quick-link anchor. (80 feet)

*Bob D'Antonio and Neil Cannon '85*

T. **Smoke Pot…Check Your Knot** *5.10b* ****

Excellent sport route over stellar features! The first sport route right of all the Arch climbs, technique past three bolts to the overlap, then take the gorgeous, interesting slab above past a high crux to obvious anchors. Must do route of the area!

8 bolts. Quick-link anchor. (80 feet)

*Bob D'Antonio*

U. **Fashionably Uninvited** *5.10c* ***

A popular, quality mixed route. Start up the first three bolts of *Smoke Pot,* and then cut left to join the long, under-cling crack which angles up and left for 80 feet to the arête. Make technical moves right around the arête past one bolt, then up and left to a set of anchors. Interesting climbing! **Use a 70m rope to rappel!**

4 bolts, cams and nuts to 2.5". Quick-link anchor. (120 feet)

*Bob D'Antonio*

V. **Inner Space Arch** *5.9* *

A varied adventure! This line takes the obvious crack forming the right side of the arch up and left to pull a roof and angle to the top, and has many variations or anchor belay set-ups to choose from.

**Pitch 1:** (5.9): Begin on the left crack that defines the right side of the major arch system. Angle up through the left facing dihedral, through the thin and slightly over grown crack all the way up left, under the roof and build a belay below the roof, where it offers the easiest looking path over the system. Bring a lot of slings to reduce rope drag. It is also possible to belay off of the anchors of *Most Toppest* (most people just do that route as a first pitch).
***Variation:*** *(5.10c)* cut up and right at the blocky feature to clip one bolt and join *Fashionably Uninvited* and clip its anchors. (100 feet)
Cams and nuts to 4". No anchor. (130 feet)
**Pitch 2:** (5.7) Climb over the small crux roof, head directly up through a small overlap, walk off left after a hundred feet or climb a short pitch (5.6) to the summit. This makes for a long, varied pitch with interesting gear and some run-outs, all which don't make it that worthwhile.
Small wires and cams to 2.5". No anchor. (130 feet)
Cams and nuts to 4". No anchor. (260 total feet)

*The next three routes are approached by a short jaunt up the low-angle slab and climb the face below the large capping roof…*

**W.** **Escorndido** *5.10a* **

A quality route on the right side of the arch. Take the awesome "rib" features up and right, then weave back left through crazy, technical moves up bulbous features to a shared anchor with *Junior Jules.*
6 bolts. Three bolt rappel anchor. (50 feet)
*Bill Schmausser and Britt Anderson*

**X.** **Junior Jules Doinks a Digit** *5.10b* ***

Great climbing up a harder-than-it-looks-start, to a run-out after the second bolt. Edge through hollow sounding flakes up and right to a high, height dependant crux. Easy climbing leads to shared anchors with *Escorndido.*
6 bolts. Three bolt rappel anchor. (40 feet)
*Bill Schmausser and Jules Van de Hei*

**Y.** **Most Toppest** *5.7* ***

A well protected slab route up awesome features on the left side of the arch. A crux at the after the third bolt is the only real slowing point in an otherwise quick and easy jug haul!
6 bolts. Quick-link anchors. (50 feet)
*Bill Schmausser and Britt Anderson*

*30 feet to the left of the arch slab, there lies one small route up the very low-angle ramp…*

**Z.** **The Welcoming** *5.4* **

A great, super easy, and well protected beginner lead on the slab left of the major arch. The easiest sport route in all of Elevenmile, and a good warm-up for the rest of the sport pitches in this area.
9 bolts. Rap ring anchor. (40 feet)
*Bill Schmausser and Britt Anderson '05*

# Messenger Wall

*[Located on the east side of the gulch, behind Turret Dome, across the river at 4.2 miles.]*

Discovered in 2005 by Stewart Green, Brian Shelton, and Bob D'Antonio, the Messenger Wall offers a variety interesting features and pitches on a vast 200 foot dome of quality granite. Hidden high on the hillside behind its brother Turret Dome, it is easy to find solitude and long routes away from the hustle and bustle of the rest of the canyon.

**Approach:** Park at the Messenger Gulch picnic site on the south side of the road. Wade the river, aiming for the obvious large valley where Turret Dome (and Messenger Wall) sits high on the east hillside. Hike up the hill, taking the path of least resistance, to the bathtub riddled wall which is where *Slippery When Wet* (Route A) is located. **Alternate:** Park at the Turret Dome picnic area and head up river along the social trails that cut west from the picnic areas. Skirt around the base of the Solar Slabs of Turret Dome, and follow the cliff line as it wraps back north uphill toward the large arch on Turret dome's west face. As the trail levels out and Turret Dome peters out, the Messenger Wall (with its large obvious bathtub features) will be visible further along the ridge. Walk along the base of the cliff past the bathtubs to the first route, *Slippery When Wet.*

*After traversing along the base of the large bathtub riddled face, at the far left end of the bathtubs (listed from right to left) are…*

**A.** **Slippery When Wet** *5.8* ***

Follow the obvious easy crack to the ledge on the far left side of the obvious large water pods that dominate the south side of the cliff. Angle up and right through a bolt protected crux bulge to the thin seam that follows bathtubs and two more bolts to high anchors at the "X" seams. Long and interesting route! **Use two 60m ropes for rappel!**

3 bolts, small wires, and cams to 2". Chain anchors. (190 feet)
*Stewart Green*

**B.** **Archangel** *5.10a* ****

Start left of *Slippery* following two bolts to a shared ledge with that route. Take the face directly up through the crux which leads to sustained 5.9 climbing up the slab past interesting features which lead to a splitter crack over a bulge to anchors. Long, varied climbing and great exposure! **Use two 60m ropes for rappel!**

12 bolts, .5" and 2" cams. Chain anchors. (190 feet)
*Stewart Green*

C. **Don't Kill the Messenger** *5.10a* **

A direct start to the first pitch of *The Messenger*. Climb the line of bolts directly up the technical face and join the left facing dihedral crack, which leads up to anchors over the small roof. A nice challenging start to the *Messenger* if you're climbing at the grade.

3 bolts, Cams to 3". Chain anchors. (100 feet)

*Bill Schmausser*

D. **The Messenger** *5.7* **

A long varied pitch up a nice line on the right side of the cliff, can be linked into one mega pitch with long slings and a double rack.

**Pitch 1:** (5.7) Begin 20 feet left of *Archangel* and climb the easy slab past three bolts, leading to a long sustained left facing flake with excellent gear to anchors over a small roof above the ledge.

3 bolts, nuts and cams to 3". (100 feet)

**Pitch 2:** (5.7) Angle up the nice, easier crack riddled face to pull a final left trending crux over the headwall, then take the easy 5.2 gully up and right to build an anchor at the summit. Walk off the backside of the cliff.

Nuts and cams to 3". (100 feet)

3 bolts, small wires, and cams to 2". Chain anchors. (190 feet)

*Brian Shelton and Stewart Green*

E. **Put it in Perspective** *5.9+****

Begin up the first three bolts of *The Messenger*. Easy climbing up nice features leads to a brief technical crux at 2/3 height. A fun, varied lead!

8 bolts. Chain anchors. (100 feet)

*Bill Schmausser*

F. **Avatar** *5.10c* **

Climb the cruxy technical corner 20 feet left of *The Messenger* to a ledge. Continue up good cracks to a red point crux over a small roof which yields easier climbing to the anchors.

8 bolts, nuts and Cams to 3". Chain anchors. (100 feet)

*The next set of routes are located 40 feet left of Avatar, off a boulder below a right facing dihedral, under two adjacent pine trees….*

G. **Seraphim** *5.10c* **

**Pitch 1** (5.10c) Climb the long, varied slab up and right off the boulder past red hangers to a technical crux at mid height. Finish through the red point crux roof to shared anchors.

7 bolts. Rappel anchors. (100 feet)

**Pitch 2** (5.6) This pitch is called *Hermes* and takes the slab on the far right side of the ledge (you may want to traverse over and build a gear station) adjacent to the left facing dihedral to high anchors on a ledge near the summit.

2 bolts, nuts and cams to 3″. Rappel anchors. (90 feet)

H. **Cherubim** *5.10a* **

Take the slab just left of the right facing corner past tenuous moves to join the face and a crack, which leads over the lip to shared anchors with the first pitch of *Seraphim.* You can alternately start the route by climbing the right facing corner as well at 5.8.

4 bolts, nuts and cams to 3″. Rappel anchors. (90 feet)

I. **Angel Wings** *5.8* **

**Pitch 1** (5.8) Begin up the slab 10 feet left of *Cherubim* and aim for an off-width crack crux which leads up varied crack systems to the ledge where the tree anchor is.

Nuts and Cams to 4″. Tree Anchor. (90 feet)

**Pitch 2** (5.9) This pitch is called *Ariel's Delight* and takes the line of bolts off the ledge over the small face (crux), to a long varied slab protected by bolts and gear to the anchors on the middle of a ledge near the summit.

5 bolts, nuts and cams to 3″. Rappel anchors. (90 feet)

*The next few routes are located 80 feet to the left of Angel Wings, and are found by looking for bolts up a right facing dihedral…*

J. **Infamous Angel** *5.7* *

**Pitch 1** (5.7) Climb up and left of the technical right facing dihedral past varied bulbous features to the ledge and build a belay at the trees.
4 bolts, Nuts and Cams to 3". Tree Anchor. (70 feet)

**Pitch 2** (5.9) Take the line of bolts off the ledge over a horn to a slab. Weave your way up past a high crux before the ledge which yields the anchors. *Variation:* This pitch is called *Drillin Billy's Booty* and takes the overhanging hand crack on the right side of the ledge to the face above past multiple overlaps (and cruxes) to shared anchors with *Infamous.* This variation takes double cams to 3".
7 bolts, nuts and cams to 3". Rappel anchors. (95 feet)

*The next few routes begin 90 feet left of Infamous Angel below a right trending ramp which leads to Pitch 1 of that route. The next two routes begin by scrambling up the ramp and building a belay at the tree…*

K. **Finding Whiskey** *5.10d* *

Begin in front of the large thin pine tree that splits the ledge in half, and climb the easy slab up to a the crux roof which gains another slightly harder slab. Finish the pitch via a red point crux over the right trending roof and traverse left to share anchors with *My Little Angel.*
Double rack of nuts and cams to 3". Rappel anchors. (90 feet)

L. **My Little Angel** *5.8* **

Decent climbing up the slab on the left side of the ledge past two bolts to a crux roof. Sustained slab climbing leads to anchors at the short headwall near the summit.
2 bolts, Double rack of nuts and cams to 3". Rappel anchors. (110 feet)

M. **Mike and Allie** *5.7*

Climb the dirty crack on the far left side of the cliff, adjacent to a right facing corner. Continue over the lip to a small tree, and either belay here or link into a long, mega pitch to shared anchors with *My Little Angel.* **You must use a 70m rope to link this pitch!**
Double rack of nuts and cams to 3". Rappel anchors. (120 feet)

# The Sentinel

*[Located high on the south hillside, on the east side of the gulch at 4.3 miles]*

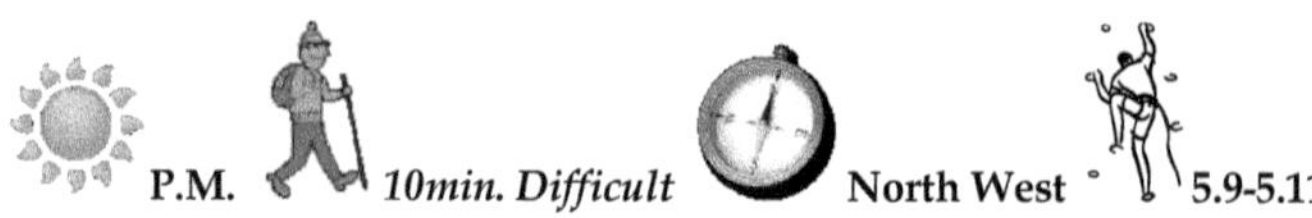


High on the hillside to the south of its larger brother Turret Dome, the Sentinel hosts several fine routes, and also offers some of the best views in the canyon. Although there was talk of an obscure traditional line out one the crag's many cracks, it wasn't until Bill Schmausser began development in '05 that the crag reached its true potential.

**Approach:** Park in the *Messenger Gulch* pullout on the left south side of the road at 4.4 miles. Hike up the hillside through the east side of the gulch, and then cut directly up to the cliff. There's no trail (as is typical with many of these areas!) so use your best judgment and just keep the cliff visible to the left, and you should be fine.

*At the far right side of the cliff, the prominent arête marks the first of the six routes listed from right to left…*

**A.** **Gran Tourismo Two** *5.11a* ****

This gorgeous, long classic takes the prominent, beautiful arête past sustained climbing and multiple cruxes to a high anchor. A midway rappel station allows easy access to those with a 50m rope.
15 bolts. Chain anchors. (120 feet)
*Bill Schmausser*

*Scramble up and left for 15 feet to a ledge, on the right side of the ledge is…*

**B.** **Gran Tourismo One** *5.11a* ***

Take the line of bolts past an incredible flake feature that runs up the steep wall. Sustained, pumpy, and interesting. Nothing else like it at Elevenmile!
8 bolts. Chain anchors. (50 feet)
*Bill Schmausser*

**C.** **The Sentinel** *5.9* **

Pleasant crack climbing that reaches the true summit of the crag.
**Pitch 1:** (5.9) Begin 15 feet left of *GT1* and take the splitter crack up the right facing dihedral for a long pitch to build a belay up and left on a ledge, under a small roof with multiple, left trending cracks. Nuts and cams to 3". No anchors. (70 feet)
**Pitch 2:** (5.6) Angle up left off the belay to a large right facing flake. Take this up to the summit, belay off a tree, then walk off the backside of the cliff. Tree anchor. (60 feet)
Nuts and cams to 3". (130 feet)
*Bill Schmausser*

D. **Zip** *5.9 ***

On a panel of its own, angle up and left, off the ledge through nice face moves and technical climbing to anchors over the lip. A good warm up for the rest of the routes in the area.

8 bolts. Chain anchors. (50 feet)

*Bill Schmausser*

E. **Thinner** *5.10c ***

Take the ultra thin face up the next panel to the left off the ledge. Seemingly endless thin crimping and edging up and left to a high anchor.

9 bolts. Chain anchors. (70 feet)

*Bill Schmausser*

F. **Kriegsmarine** *5.10b *****

It's hard to find more varied climbing than this! Take the furthest sport route left up through multiple engaging slab moves, two roofs, and cracks, all of which comprise a must do quality route!

6 bolts. Chain anchors. (60 feet)

*Bill Schmausser*

# The Sports Crag

*[Located midway uphill and across the river on the north side of the road at 4.8 miles]*

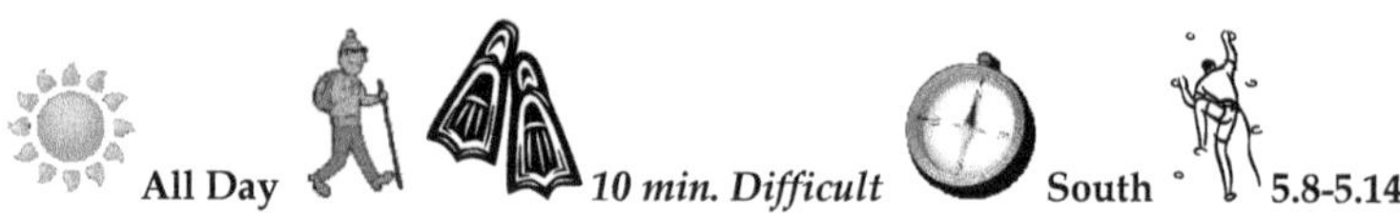


The Sports crag hosts some of the most superb, hard crack climbing in the canyon and has the best concentration of steep, splitter cracks in all of Elevenmile. Known by many as "Bob's hard man crag," this wall boasts many incredible routes that have good protection. This crag was made famous in 1982 when Australian climber Chris Peisker climbed *Albatross* (5.12d), showing the cutting edge of difficulty that could be achieved with modern camming gear. While Bob D'Antonio developed the majority of the crag's other hard routes, (some of the 5.12s ground up on site!) there still resides a tremendous amount of opportunity for quality hard climbs!

**Approach:** Park beneath the Teal Tower and walk east along the road for 150' to a shallow river crossing on your left, in the eddy behind two large boulders. Wade the river, and head northeast up the hill toward the beautifully colored, steep, and splitter crack riddled face, with the obvious bath tub sized water pods at the top. A double rack up to a 3" cam will get you up every route there.

*On the far left side of the cliff, in an alcove, this beautiful wall host two decent routes…*

**A.** **Ecstasy and Wise Guys** *5.11c* *

Long moves, poor feet, and deceptively harder than it looks from the ground, this re-bolted r/x route has a difficult start (recommended stick clip), followed by easier ground to anchors in the groove.
5 bolts. Cold shut anchor. (40 feet)
*Bob D'Antonio '82*

**B.** **Moon Age Daydreaming** *5.12b R* *

This technical left facing dihedral will test your mental tenacity and footwork, with a crux down low, past an old SMC hanger, to flaring gear above. Hard moves to much easier climbing.
1 bolt, pro to 3". No anchor. (40 feet)
*Mark Rolofson '83*

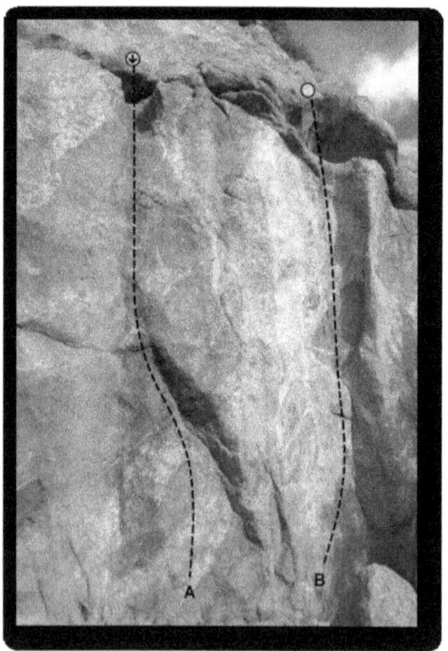

*Down and right around the corner on the main face of the crag…*

C. **Albatross** *5.12d* ***

The one and only! A.K.A. Peisker crack, very difficult technical finger jamming for the first 20 feet, to a knee-bar rest below the pin. Recompose for a pumpy technical finish.

Medium nuts, and finger sized cams to 2". Rap bolts. (55 feet)

*Chris Peisker '82*

D. **Shock the Monkey** *5.12a* ****

Incredibly fun, dynamic climbing on excellent rock, this roof crack will test your endurance on perfect hands and jugs all the way until the end with great placements exactly where you need them. If you're just breaking into hard traditional climbing, do this route!

Double cams to 3 ". Rap bolts. (50 feet)

*Bob D'Antonio '82*

E. **Fiddler Under the Roof** *5.11a* *

This slightly crumbly, technical mixed route follows the crack up and right under the roof to finish at hidden anchors right over the lip. Cool position, old school pro.

Three pins ,TCU's, and nuts (mostly small). Ring anchors. (35 feet)

F. **Open Project** *5.14-* ***

While this hairline seem has been top roped, it will take a mutant to hold on and place gear on this 5.14 crack.

TCU's and micro wires. No anchor. (40 feet)

G. **Open Project** *5.13-* ***

The overhanging, under-cling system that juts up and left from *Desmund*. Juggy climbing leads to a dynamic crux, which is hard to protect as it goes to the top. Medium to large cams and nuts. No Anchor. (55 feet)

H. **Desmond Dyno** *5.12a* **

Fun, steep, and gymnastic climbing with a hard but well-protectable crux down low. The top has some of the best steep jugs in Elevenmile! Easy to protect until the very end.

Medium cams and nuts, then bigger cams to 4". Cold shut anchor. (40 feet)

*Bob D'Antonio '84*

I. **The Leaner** *5.10c* ****

A bouldery start opens to an amazing finger crack, lie-backing on the left facing, over-hanging corner. Easier climbing to chicken heads at the lip. A long, fun climb that makes a great warm-up for the others at the crag.

Cams to 2", double the finger sizes. Chain anchor. (80 feet)

*Russ Johnson '82*

*Just right around the corner…*

**J.** **Trout Fishing in America** *5.8 R* **

Start just left of *Warm-up Corner*, following a very juggy but run-out section for 20 feet until you reach the black crack that snakes its way up to finish 5 feet left of *Warm-up Corner*. Originally soloed!

Cams to 2". No anchor. (50 feet)

*Bob D'Antonio '83*

**K.** **Warm-up Corner** *5.8* ***

Exceptionally fun and sustained crack climbing up the right facing dihedral. Engaging stemming with good pro, makes this a great intro for the aspiring trad leader!

Bring the whole rack, every size cam to 5" on this one! No anchor. (50 feet)

*Russ Johnson '82*

**L.** **Concrete Slippers** *5.11a R/X*

Scary! Decent, but extremely dangerous climbing past two old SMC hangers. If you do this, it is a recommended top rope!

2 bolts. No anchor. (40 feet)

*Bob D'Antonio '84*

# Teale Tower

*[Located across the river on the north side of the road at 5.1 miles]*

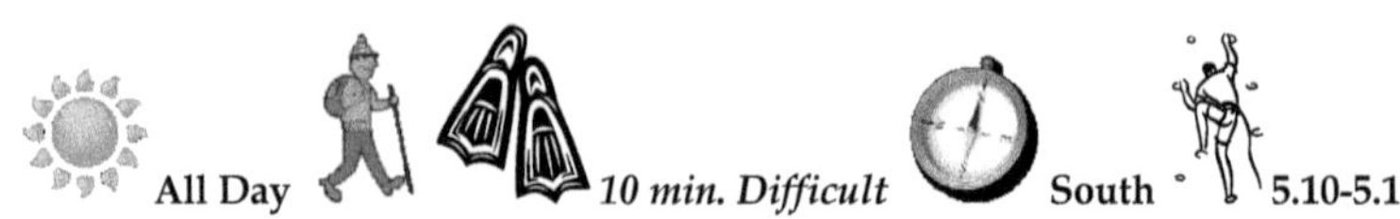


This striking formation was a major player in the history of ethics for development of Elevenmile Canyon. Home to the classic *Teale Tower Route* which was first put up in 1979 by Peter Gallager and Peter Williams, this striking line opened the eyes of climbers to the quality potential of hard climbing the canyon had to offer. In 1984 ground up standards continued to prevail, when Darryl Roth and Richard Aschert established *Run For Your Life*. According to legend, Roth, who was on red-point loaded down with bolt gear, climbed almost 40 feet of tenuous and hairy climbing above the last bolt Aschert had put in. Praying for a spot he could place his next bolt, he could not let go at a single place in the blank dihedral to drill. The route got its name as Darryl ran for his life to the ledge, and vowed to never bolt on lead again. He also gave permission to add bolts to the route, giving testament to Darryl's humble ego to make a route safe and fun for the next party, rather than put up death routes to prove how bold a climber he was. Many of the routes here have old school ratings, so enjoy the history of each route as you embark on an adventure through Elevenmile Canyon's past.

**Approach:** Park at the pullout directly across the river from the dome at 5.0 miles. Either wade the river directly to the crag, or walk up to the bridge near the Springer Gulch campground and take the opposite bank back downstream to the crag.

***A.*** **The Off-width** *5.11c*

**Pitch 1** (5.7): Follow any of the easy cracks up to the ledge, all variations are between 5.7 and 5.9. Small to medium cams and stoppers. Build an anchor at the ledge. (30 feet)
**Pitch 2** (5.11c): Launch into the overhanging, fist to off-width crack. Strenuous! It may be a little dirty in places, so a brush might also help. Bring all your bigger cams, doubles from fist up to 6″. Build an anchor over the ledge at the same place as Teale Tower Route. (50 feet)
**Pitch 3** (5.9): The big tiered roofs above are nowhere near as intimidating as they look; in fact, this pitch is the icing on the cake of the whole route! From the station head up through the overlaps, using jugs to traverse the roofs. Bring LOTS of long slings for this pitch to minimize rope drag. Small nuts and cams to 1.5″, build an anchor at the ledge on the summit. (70 feet)
Bring the whole rack, all size nuts and cams to 6″. No anchors. (130 feet)

A
B
C
D
ABCD
E

**B.** **Teale Tower Route** *5.11a* ****

The area classic! Don't miss this route if you're looking for sustained crack climbing on great stone. Old school and very hard for the grade!

**Pitch 1** (5.8): Follow any of the easy cracks up to the ledge; all variations are between 5.7 and 5.9. Cams and nuts to 3". Build an anchor at the ledge. (30 feet)

**Pitch 2** (5.11a): From the ledge, head up and right over fins and crimps to the obvious overhanging finger crack. Clip the fixed nut, and crank through the technical tips crux to a sinker hand jam where the crack begins to widen. The climbing gradually eases off for the next 50 feet, as the crack gets wider. Bring the full rack, doubles of finger size nuts and cams to 2", and a couple of bigger cams to 5" for the upper crack. Build an anchor on the ledge. (80 feet)

**Pitch 3** (5.8): The big tiered roofs above are nowhere near as intimidating as they look; in fact, this pitch is the icing on the cake of the whole route! From the station head up through the overlaps, using jugs to traverse the roofs. Bring LOTS of long slings for this pitch to minimize rope drag. Small nuts and cams to 1.5", build an anchor at the ledge on the summit. (70 feet)

Doubles cams and nuts to 2", and singles to 5". No anchors. (180 total feet)

*Peter Gallagher, Pete Williams '79*

**C.** **Run For Your Life** *5.11a R/X* **

Great climbing, but if you fall you will most likely die. This is the route that made Darryl stop bolting on lead, and for good reason! There's nothing to hold on to, let alone hook to put in bolts!

**Pitch 1** (5.8): Follow any of the easy cracks up to the ledge. All variations are between 5.7 and 5.9. Cams and Stoppers to 3". Build an anchor at the ledge. (30 feet)

**Pitch 2** (5.11a): Starting off the same ledge as the previous two routes, head up and right placing marginal gear in the flakes and clip the first bolt. If you have a death wish, climb past this bolt into great technical moves on micro smears and run for your life up the flaring dihedral to the ledge.

3 bolts. No anchor. (75 feet)

**Pitch 3** (5.8): The big tiered roofs above are nowhere near as intimidating as they look. This pitch is the icing on the cake of the whole route! From the station head up through the overlaps, using jugs to traverse the roofs. Bring LOTS of long slings for this pitch to minimize rope drag.

Small nuts and cams to 1.5". Build an anchor at the ledge on the summit. (70 feet)

Double cams and nuts to 2", 3 bolts. No anchors, (180 total feet)

*Darryl Roth '84*

D. **Candidate for Space** *5.11b R* ***

This route offers incredible position and great moves up the right side of the cliff. You'll want to be prepared for this one, with its exposure, hard climbing, and long run-outs over marginal gear, this route is no joke.

**Pitch 1** (5.9): Start just right of the panel of stone that the previous routes climb, and take any crack system that looks easy up to the ledge system right of *Run for Your Life*. Build an anchor where it's comfortable to start the next pitch.

Full rack up to 2". No Anchor. (40 feet)

**Pitch 2** (5.11b R): Take the flake systems up the long, varied panel. This pitch has stunning position, and takes some great features up the exposed face. The R rating comes from the run-outs between the flakes. Build an anchor over the lip in a scoop dihedral feature.

Nuts and cams to 2". No Anchor. (90 feet)

**Pitch 3** (5.8): Climb up and right through a small roof, and take crack systems to the summit. Build a belay at an easy walk off point.

Nuts and cams to 3". No Anchor. (60 feet)

E. **Reality Check** *5.10c* ***

A quality moderate up the right side of the cliff, and a good route to get up the tower for those not quite ready for *Teal Tower Route.*

**Pitch 1** (5.9): Climb the easiest looking dihedral crack system 15 feet left of a low roof feature to build a belay at the ledge.

Full rack up to 2". No Anchor. (40 feet)

**Pitch 2** (5.10c): Climb the large dihedral systems off the belay through interesting features and intriguing moves to build a belay on the left side of a left facing corner.

Nuts and cams to 2". No Anchor. (90 feet)

**Pitch 3** (5.7): Climb up and right through the crack system out a small roof to a much easier crack system that leads to the summit. Build a belay at an easy walk off point, heading east down the right side of the crag.

Nuts and cams to 3". No Anchor. (60 feet)

*Darryl Roth and Kim Steiner '83*

# Springer Gulch

*[Located above the Springer Gulch Campground at 5.2 miles]*

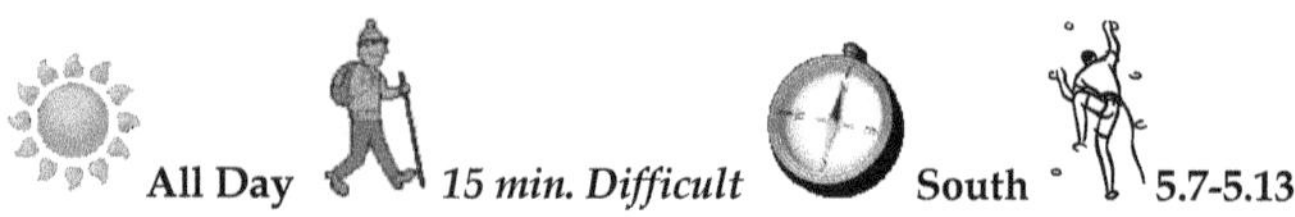


Only one word can describe the Springer Gulch area, HUGE. This massive south facing cliff band sits high on the hillside like a massive castle overlooking the entirety of Elevenmile, and has one of the best settings of any crag in the canyon. Hosting sport routes, mixed climbs, and stellar cracks from 5.7 to 5.13, this place is hard to beat if you're only visiting for a short while. The climbing here was developed by the usual suspects of Glenn Schuler, Kevin McLaughlin, Bob D'Antonio, and Bill Schmuasser, and gained a significant amount of popularity due to the well bolted sport routes of the area. Have fun!

**Approach:** There are a number of ways to access this cliff, but the most popular is to park at the gate (if you are not already paying for camping) and take the hiking trail near the entrance up the hillside, then cut north and walk uphill toward the cliff. Aim for the area you plan to climb, but the most common trails deposit you near the Sunkist area.

*On the far left side of the entire complex…*

## Little Kingdom

The leftmost sector of Springer Gulch, this small cliff band has three worthwhile routes. The Little Kingdom cull-du-sac is located downhill and left of the Future cul-du-sac, 50 feet past the small boulder field that sits in front of that crag.

**A.** **Statement for Youth** *5.12a* ***

In the dihedral just left of the *Little Kingdom* slab, this route takes good rock up the right angling overhanging dihedral to a crux stemming move, then cut up left past one more bolt through sloping, lie-backs to anchors. Sustained for how short it is!
3 bolts, cams to 1.5". Tree anchor. (35 feet)
*Bob D' Antonio and Richard Aschert*

**B.** **Little Kingdom** *5.13a* **

This historic test piece takes the prominent micro-crack riddled panel up and right through sustained 5.12 to a crux at the third bolt, then angle back up left via a sloping arête and mantle to a dead tree for an anchor over the lip. This route feels old school.
3 bolts. Tree anchor. (35 feet)
*Bob D'Antonio '86*

C. **Here's Two Old Flakes** *5.11c* **

This short but quality crack climb takes the left start to the obvious arch right of *Little Kingdom.* Easy, pumpy, lie-back moves up right lead to a crux pulling the overhanging crack that angles back up left. Good quality stone.
Cams to 3". No Anchor. (40 feet)
*Mark Milligan '86*

*About 80 feet uphill, east along the cliff, scramble up through a small boulder field heading through a small valley to…*

## The Future Cul-Du-Sac

About 50 feet left of the Back Street Wall, this small cove of routes is accessed by means of walking through a small boulder field to gain a hanging valley of a few decent routes. Listed from left to right…

D. **Escape to the Future** *5.11b* **

On the far left side of the west facing wall, this route takes the obvious right leaning crack up the overhanging, shallow dihedral to exit via crux up and left to join a crack that goes left around the corner.
Cams and nuts to 3". No Anchor. (50 feet)
*Bob D'Antonio '86*

E. **Here's to Future Ways** *5.12b* **

Starting the same as *Escape,* follow the crack up and right to an interesting hand traverse and a thin boulder problem (past a bolt) to top out on the lip. This was a very popular route for hard men in the '80s, but now sees little traffic.
1 bolt, cams and nuts to 3". No Anchor. (50 feet)
*Bob D' Antonio*

*Hike for another 80 yards to where the cliff line becomes less broken up and more consistent, here you will come to a large slab with huge capping roofs, this is…*

## The Back Street Wall

Beneath the obvious capping roof that sits like a barrette over the slabs (that are just left of the Intimidator Roof) this wall hosts nine decent moderate routes. All routes here were developed by Stewart Green, Brian Shelton, and Mike Heinricks.

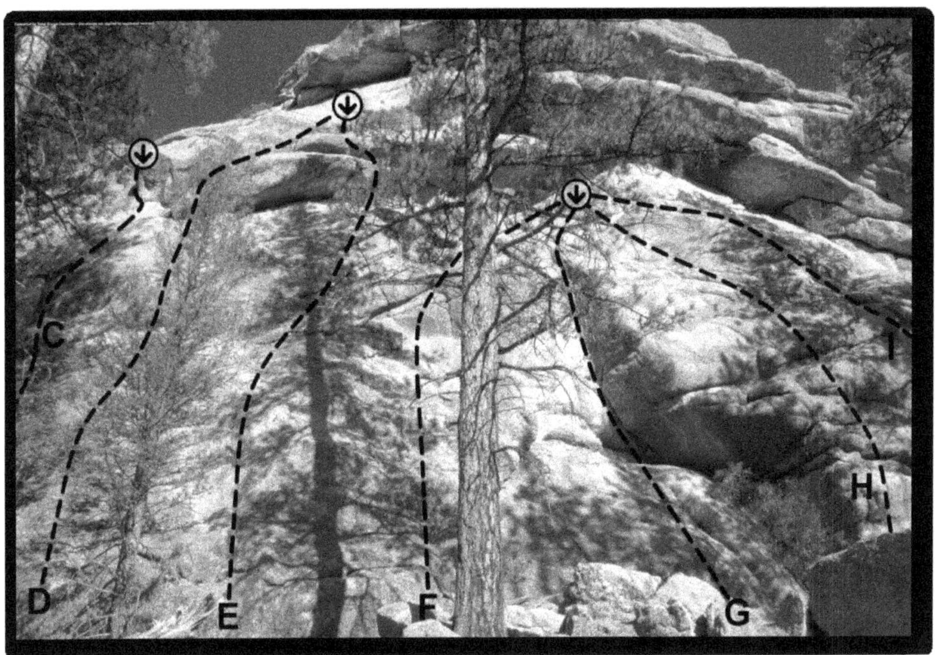


**A.** **Camino Real** *5.10d* **

On the far left side of the crag, climb over a large tufa rib feature to a ledge, and either build a belay here, or link it as one long pitch with runners through the off-width dihedral feature up top. Walk off the back side. No topo.
Nuts and cams to 6". No Anchor. (160 feet)

**B.** **My Next 30 Years** *5.8* **

15 feet right of *Camino Real* climb the crack through a water groove to an obvious dihedral. Climb the dihedral through a crux, then angle up right to anchors shared with *Down the Allie,* and finish the optional second pitch of that route. No topo.
Nuts and cams to 2". Rappel anchor. (160 feet)

C. **Down the Allie** *5.9* ***

Climb the water groove on the left side of the arches to a slot with another red point crux through the thin finger crack. Finish the pitch through an easy pull to a rappel anchor at the break, or continue up long, easy slabs trending left to build an anchor at the summit.

Nuts and cams to 2". Rappel anchor. (150 feet)

D. **Taiwan Tango** *5.10b* **

Climb past a low crux to an easier face which leads to the left most side of the roof systems and the main arch. Pull another crux over the roof, and continue up a crack system to shared anchors with *Third World Cantina.*

5 Bolts. Small nuts and cams to 2". Chain Anchor. (60 feet)

E. **Third World Cantina** *5.10d* ***

To the left of *Pine Lane* and right of a small fir tree, climb the shiny line of six bolts to a crux roof, and finish up the easier crack to anchors below the next roof system.

6 Bolts. Nuts and Cams to 3". Rappel Anchor. (100 feet)

F. **Pine Lane** *5.6***

Ten feet left of the dihedral, climb the discontinuous flake systems up the middle of the face past decent gear, then cut up right to community anchors via the right trending train track cracks.

Nuts and Cams to 3". Ring Anchor. (65 feet)

G. **A Street** *5.10b* **

In the middle of the arches, edge your way to the crack in the left facing corner, jam through the roof, and slab climb to the community anchors below the roof.

2 Bolts, medium to large cams to 4". Ring Anchor. (60 feet)

H. **Get High Street** *5.9+* **

Starting immediately left of *Fast Lane (*right of the left facing dihedral), and climb through a low, height dependant crux to easier slab climbing past three bolts to the community anchor below the roof.

3 Bolts, small nuts and cams to 2". Ring anchor. (65 feet)

I. **Anything But the Fast Lane** *5.8* **

On the right side of the crag, start behind a large pine tree, and pull a low crux over a roof to angle up left across the slab to a community anchor station below the main roof of the arches.

Nuts and cams to 3". Ring Anchor. (70 feet)

## The Intimidator Roof

Immediately right of the Back Street Wall lies this impressive wall, hosting an assortment of fine routes.

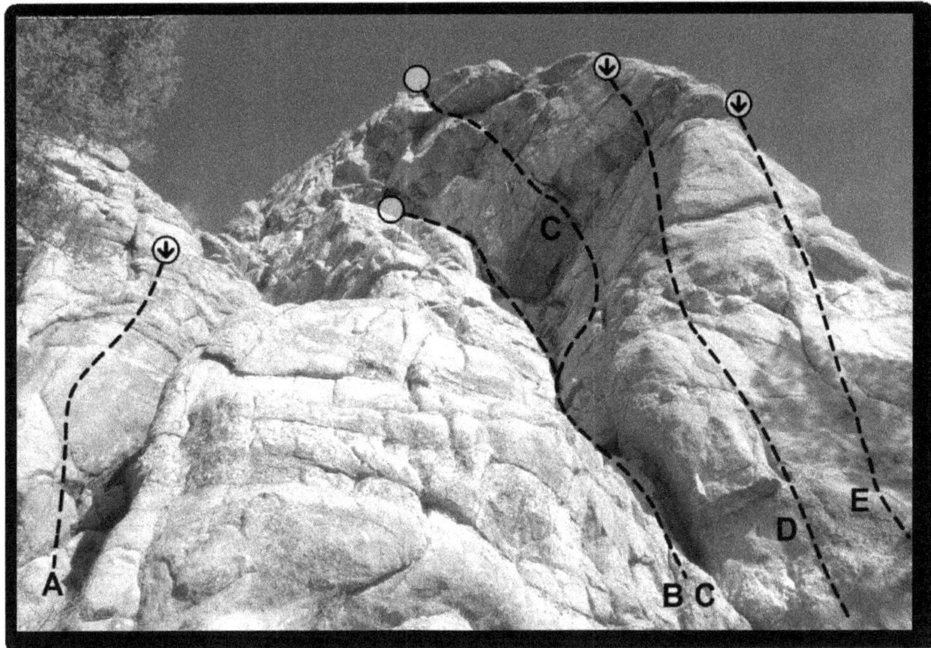


A. **Unknown** *5.10* **

The first route on the slabs right of the *Backstreet Wall,* climb bolts past a dihedral onto a technical face. Take easier slabs and cracks to anchors.
7 bolts. Rappel Anchor. (80 feet)

B. **Gear Climb** *5.10* *

Take the obvious, increasingly lower angle dihedral crack running under the Intimidator face, up and left to a break where a rotten white sling is the only remnant of an anchor.
Nuts and Cams to 4". No Anchor. (90 feet)

C. **The Intimidator** *5.12d* ****

The name does it justice, as this obvious splitter crack is the only feature up the towering overhanging panel. Climb the easy dihedral and cut up right (when convenient) across the slab, to join the start of roof crack that leads to a dynamic V5 boulder problem surmounting the lip. Take the crack up through easier, harder to protect territory to the summit, or traverse right to *McLaughling's* anchors. **You Will Need a 70 Meter Rope to Rappel.**
Nuts and Cams to 3". No Anchor. (120 feet)

D. **McLaughling** *5.12d* **

Climb the prominent line up bolts up the easy slab past a small roof, which leads to a well protected roof crux up high. Sustained crimping over the clean exposed panel leads to anchors. Great position! **You Will Need a 70 Meter Rope to Rappel.**
10 bolts. Chain Anchor. (100 feet)
*Kevin McLaughlin and Glenn Schuler '93*

E. **Surfing With the Alien** *5.12a* ***

This well known arête classic is top ten on most Elevenmile climber's lists. Technical, wild position and varied climbing characterize this interesting line. Sling a chicken head to protect the start moves, and then fire up to a crux bulge just above the fixed rotten sling. The rock is a little flakey, but will clean up with more traffic.
9 bolts. Chain anchor. (90 feet)
*Glenn Schuler '92*

F. **Bill & Britt One** *5.10a* ***

Twenty feet right of *Surfing,* climb broken looking rock between good jugs and slightly chossy rock to anchors hidden over the lip. Fun, dynamic climbing that is steeper than it looks!
3 bolts. Ring anchor. (45 feet)
*Bill Schmausser and Britt* Anderson

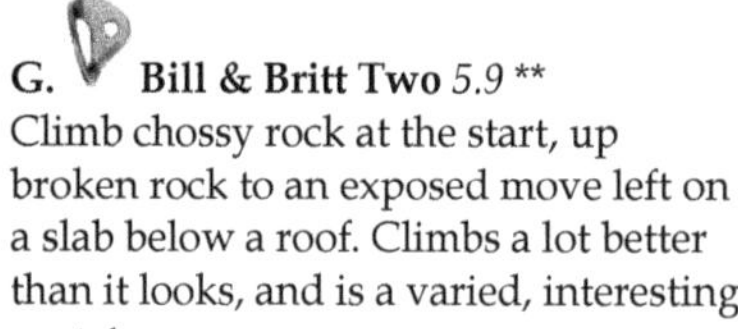

G. **Bill & Britt Two** *5.9* **
Climb chossy rock at the start, up broken rock to an exposed move left on a slab below a roof. Climbs a lot better than it looks, and is a varied, interesting route!
4 bolts. Ring anchor. (45 feet)
*Bill Schmausser and Britt* Anderson

H. **Bill & Britt Three** *5.10a* *
Up the corner, (on the left side of a roof system) climb up left through a large "chimney" to anchors at the top of the crack.
5 bolts, # 2 cam. Ring anchor. (50 feet)
*Bill Schmausser and Britt Anderson*

*Following the roof system around right, leads to a large alcove (usually the deposit point of the trails from the parking) which is called…*

## The Sunkist Alcove

**A.** **Open Project** *5.13* **

On the prominent arête, this beautiful line has thwarted the attempts of a handful of talented climbers, and will be an area test piece when completed. Climb up and left past a stud at the first bolt, then up and left over technical climbing through the bulging cruxes to anchors over the lip.
6 bolts. Chain anchor. (65 feet)
*Glenn Schuler*

**B.** **Overpower by Funk** *5.12d* ***

Up the beautiful overhanging face, take crimps and edges up to a funky crux at mid height, and then turn on the afterburners for the pumpy exit out the lie-back roof flake up high. Lower off cold shuts or traverse left to the newer chain anchors on *Project*. An old school classic!
6 bolts. Cold shut anchors. (60 feet)
*Glenn Schuler and Kevin McLaughlin '93*

*Just right of the panel on the long slabs…*

C. **Sunkist** *5.7* ***

On the left side of the slab, climb nice features up the frequently sun baked face. A great moderate pitch and a good first lead!
6 Bolts. Rappel Anchor. (60 feet)
*Glenn Schuler and Judy Schuler '92*

D. **Cleavage** *5.8* **

Another quality moderate akin to its brother *Sunkist.* Edge your way up the right side of the face, past a slight run-out at the second bolt (which may be protected by a 2.5″ cam), to a couple of run-outs over easy terrain at the top.
5 Bolts. Rappel Anchor. (70 feet)
*Glenn Schuler and Judy Schuler '92*

*30 feet right on a small overhanging prow…*

E. **Unsung Hero** *5.12b* ***

Sitting by itself, this cool looking bulge is a popular endeavor for those visiting Springer Gulch. Climb easy slabs to sustained, dynamic cruxes out the bulge with the hardest moves at the top. Easier climbing leads to anchors.
5 bolts. Chain Anchor. (50 feet)
*Mark Vanhorn*

## Face It Slab

Walk another 100 feet east along the cliff line, to a gorgeous slab. The first route, Kokopeli, resides behind a large pine on the left side of the face.

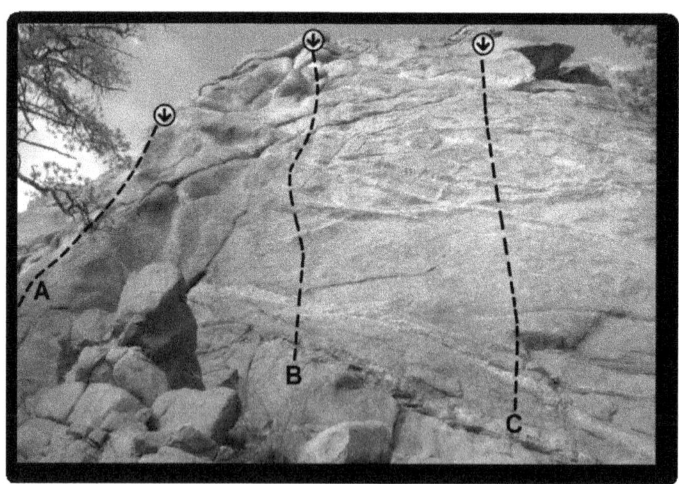

A. **Kokopeli** *5.10c* ***

Climb up the relatively easy slab to a cruxy exit off the large prow to anchors over the lip. A well protected warm up!
5 bolts. Chain Anchor. (60 feet)
*Glenn Schuler and Judy Schuler '92*

*20 feet right on the main face…*

B. **Schmausser's** *5.11b* **

Another sustained slab (with a crux at the second bolt) to cool features up high.
4 bolts. Single bolt anchor. (60 feet)
*Bill Schmausser '92*

C. **Face It** *5.12a* **

Crimp and smear up the beautiful slab past two bolts (and a crux at mid height) to sustained climbing up high on the face. Cool features!
4 bolts. Single bolt anchor. (70 feet)
*Bill Schmausser '92*

*Hike 300 feet east and up the hill to another higher cliff band and a cool wavy panel of rock known as…*

## The Scoop Wall

The Scoop Wall used to be very popular due to the quality of the routes and the well protected nature of the climbs, but has since been eclipsed by the newer, more accessible crags off the road. This is still a superb place to climb, and would be a great place to go for moderate climbing if you want to avoid the crowds.

*On the left side of the wall…*

A. **Crest of a Wave** *5.10d* **

On the far left side of the crag, climb over a low crux at the roof to very interesting moves over cool ripples and waves in the rock. The run-outs can be supplemented with good gear.
5 Bolts, small nuts and cams to 2". Chain anchor. (60 feet)

B. **Body Surfing** *5.11b* ***

Climb the crux roof of *Crest of a Wave*, then traverse right after the first bolt to clip the third bolt of *Body English* and finish up that route. Combines the best moves on both routes, and is a worthwhile linkup.
3 bolts, wires and Cams to 2". Chain Anchor. (70 feet)

C. **Body English** *5.11b* ***

Climb a desperate, low, lie-back crux out the bulge to superb climbing on great rock over a variety of interesting features.

4 bolts, wires and cams to 2". Rappel anchor. (65 feet)

*Glenn Schuler '92*

D. **Scoop DeVille** *5.10b* ****

This superb pitch was heralded as one of the best 5.10's in the canyon during the development surge in the '90s, and still maintains classic status. Excellent climbing over beautiful, wavy rock past multiple cruxes make this a must do. The bolting is a little sporty as well.

5 bolts. Rappel anchor. (70 feet)

*Brent Kertzman '85*

E. **Undertow** *5.6* **

Squeezed between *Scoop* and *Head*, this well protected, moderate pitch is a great warm-up for the rest of the routes at the crag. Steep easy climbing!

5 bolts. Chain anchor. (50 feet)

F. **Head Over Squeals** *5.9* *

The furthest right route on the wall, climb the run-out section to the first bolt and continue up varied terrain through multiple brief cruxes to a flake feature which leads to the summit, and a tree to build an anchor.

3 bolts, nuts and cams to 2". No anchor. (95 feet)

*Brent Kertzman and Gary VanDerwiede '86*

Ben Spannuth on the classic *Inception* (5.13c), Heavens Gate. Jason Pool photo.

# The River Wall

*[Located across the river on the north bank at 6.0 miles]*

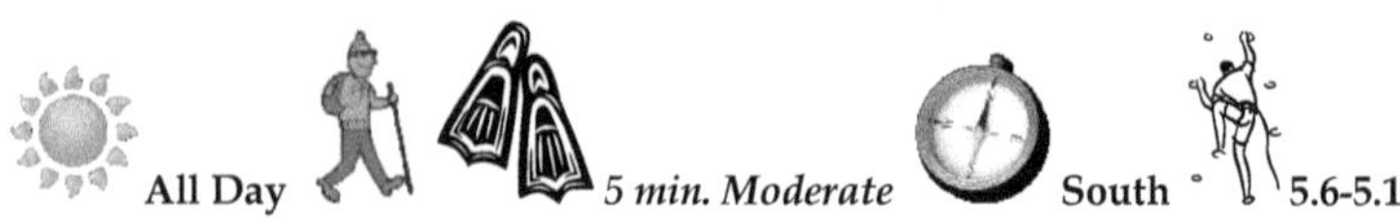


The River Wall is quintessential Elevenmile climbing. With its excellent stone, wide variety of routes at many grades, sport and traditional climbing, and its "poolside" access to the best swimming hole in the canyon, the River Wall should be one of the first on your hit list of summer crags.

*On the far left side of the cliff…*

**A.** **Parallel Universes** *5.9* **

On the far left side of the cliff, climb past a low crux over a roof, and then motor up easier climbing to the anchors.
4 bolts. Rappel anchors. (40 feet)

B. **Hebrew Hangover** *5.8 ***

Behind a large pine tree, climb past a low, crimpy crux then much easier climbing to the anchors.
4 bolts. Rappel anchors. (40 feet)

C. **Mid-Day Lightning** *5.6 ***

The rightmost of the three sport routes on the left side of the cliff. A low crux leads to a jug haul.
3 bolts. Rappel anchors. (35 feet)
*Bob D' Antonio*

D. **Bob's Solo** *5.4 **

A vague line right of the sport routes, climb a low-angle face to a shallow right facing dihedral.
Nuts and cams to 3". Tree anchor. (45 feet)
*Bob D' Antonio*

E. **Slab O' Bob** *5.6 **

Left of the small overhanging arch, climb up the face past horizontal cracks to the ledge above.
Nuts and cams to 3". Tree anchor. (45 feet)
*Bob D' Antonio*

F. **Getting Older** *5.8 ***

Left of *PBR,* this line takes the technical face under the small arch through a brief roof crack to the easy slab above. Angle up right to shared anchors with *PBR.*
Nuts and cams to 3". Rappel anchor. (40 feet)
*Bob D' Antonio*

G. **PBR Me** *5.12a ***

Hard climbing off the flaring crack between gastons, to a crux pulling over the bulge. Easier climbing to the anchors as the route slabs out.
4 bolts. Rappel anchors. (40 feet)
*Ian-Spencer Green '06*

H. **Captain Cod Piece** *5.11c **

This would be world class finger crack climbing, if it were ten times as long! Start in the finger crack just right of the right facing dihedral, and power through tip jams past a fixed wire, over a bulge where the climbing backs off significantly.
Small cams and nuts to 2". Cold shut anchors. (40 feet)
*Kevin Lindorff '84*

I. **Darylect** *5.12c ****

This stellar route is steep and powerful the whole way! Long moves between decent, small holds make up the meat of this black streaked beast. Sustained fun!
5 bolts. Cold-shut anchors. (40 feet)

*Ian Spencer Green and Darryl Roth '94*

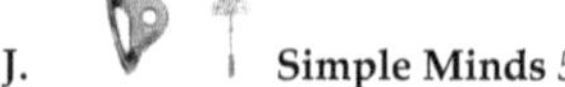

J. **Simple Minds** *5.12b **

In the cluster of trees in the middle of the cliff, climb past a bolt up a crimpy face to join a right facing crack at mid height. Continue up past two bolts to belay at a tree over the lip.

3 bolts, nuts and cams to 3". Tree anchor. (45 feet)

K. **Loaf and Jug** *5.7 **

Start on the vertical face just left of the overhanging bulge. Make moves between good jugs to gain the slab, and smear your way up to the top of the face with a crux up high. Fun moves and a good beginner traditional climb with good stone.

Full rack with nuts and cams to 3". Chain anchor. (60 feet)

*Stewart Green and Martha Morris '94*

L. **Life on the Run** *5.10a ****

Stellar crack climbing! Start in the deteriorating crack and angle up and right to the cracks heading just right of the big roof. As stone turns from moderate to supreme, make the crux move over the small roof with good, but slightly spaced protection to anchors over the lip.

Small to medium nuts and cams, take a couple cams to 3". Chain anchor. (50 feet)

*Bob D'Antonio '85*

M. **Running Man** *5.10a R* *

A vague, old school route comprised of run-out, but quality climbing. Start on *Blood Brothers* and angle up left to scale the ribs and cracks to parallel *Life on the Run.* Most of the gear is good, but far apart. The crux hits at the bulge and headwall before the long chain anchors.

Small to medium cams to 2" and nuts. Chain anchors. (50 feet)

*Bob D' Antonio and Mark Hesse '85*

N. **Blood Brothers** *5.12b* *

Climb the high angle face past crimps (placing small gear) to a rest below the bulge. Clip the bolt and fire the hard crux moves through the bulging headwall. A one move wonder! Shares anchors with *Running Man.*

1 bolt, small to medium cams and nuts. Chain anchor. (50 feet)

*Bob D' Antonio and Ian-Spencer Green '94*

O. **Flat Earth Society** *5.11c* **

This wandering route starts on the ribs about 15 feet left of the dihedral, and climbs through delicate slab moves up to the big, under-cling crack. Trend left for about 7 feet, and cut up right for more slab moves, to a crux at the bulging section. You can cut right at the last bolt for an easier finish. This route is technical, hard, and run-out!

4 bolts, nuts and cams to 2". Cold shut anchors. (65 feet)

*Ian Spencer Green '95*

P. **Pumping Chuck** *5.11b* **

This scaly route climbs better than it looks. Technical climbing over poorly placed SMC hangers takes you past a crux at the bottom, with easier climbing to the top. Crimpy and sharp, with a weird anchor placement.

3 bolts. Cold shut anchors. (35 feet)

*Bob D' Antonio and Chuck Carlson '94*

Q. **Skid Marks** *5.11d* ***

This route is a river wall classic, old school and very hard for the grade! Start with a powerful crimpy crux up the right side overhang (recommended stick clip!) to gain an awkward rest and bigger holds around the corner. Make technical moves and hard clips up the arête, and top out over the feature to the non-obvious and poor anchor placement.

5 bolts. Cold shut anchors. (40 feet)

*Bob D' Antonio and Kevin Lindorff*

# The Short Wall

*[Located across the river on the north bank at 6.4 miles]*

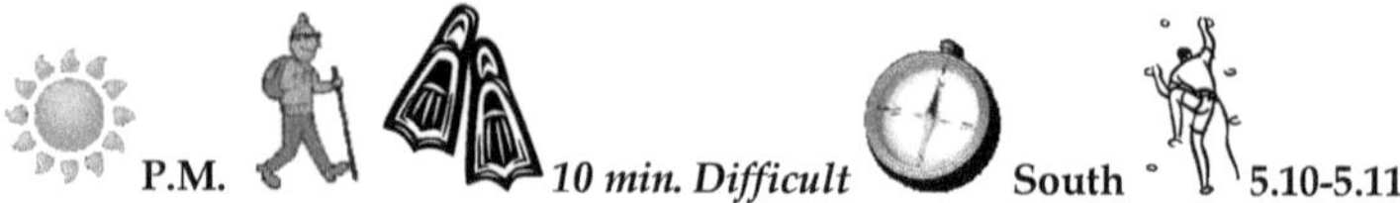


High above the popular *Murray Boulders*, the short wall has two decent routes for those traditional climbing fiends who want some more adventure.

**Approach:** Park at the pullout at 6.4 miles, and walk down the hillside to cross the river and bushwack up the hill. The approach landmark is the obvious collection of large, quality looking boulders below the wall.

**A.** **O.D.** *5.10b* **

Take the beautiful, obvious, left trending splitter crack on the left panel to the top of the cliff. Cool climbing!
Nuts and Cams to 3". No anchor. (50 feet)
*Bob D'Antonio '84*

**B.** **Race With a Demon** *5.11a* ***

Climb the striking overhanging dihedral crack that forms the main corner of the wall. A little dirty and loose.
Nuts and Cams to 3". No anchor. (50 feet)
*Bob D'Antonio and Shawn Wilson '83*

# The Spy Roof

*[Located across the river on the north bank at 6.6 miles]*

This striking riverside roof system hosts the walls namesake classic *Spy vs. Spy,* offers climbers the opportunity to break off the beaten path and try something a little different.

**Approach:** Park at any one of the pullputs near the crag, and scramble down the steep hillside, wade the river at the most shallow spot, and bushwack your way to the cliff.

**A.** **Tesuque** *5.10d* **

Climb the splitter crack system on the left side of the roof past varied face and crack climbing to the summit and build an anchor at the tree over the lip.
Nuts and Cams to 3″. No anchor. (65 feet)
*Bob D'Antonio*

B. **Spy vs. Spy** *5.12c ****

Climb the beautiful tiered roof crack past two old pitons (crux) and finish up the easier vertical crack to the summit. An Elevenmile icon test piece!

Two pins, nuts and cams to 3". No anchor. (75 feet)

*Will Gadd and Eric Harp '85*

C. **Eric's Face** *5.8**

On the right side of the cliff climb up the corner system and horizontal seams to the summit of the smaller face, build an anchor over the lip.

Nuts and cams to 3". No anchor. (50 feet)

*Eric Harp '85*

# The Indulgence Crag

## *[Located across the river on the north bank at 6.7 miles]*

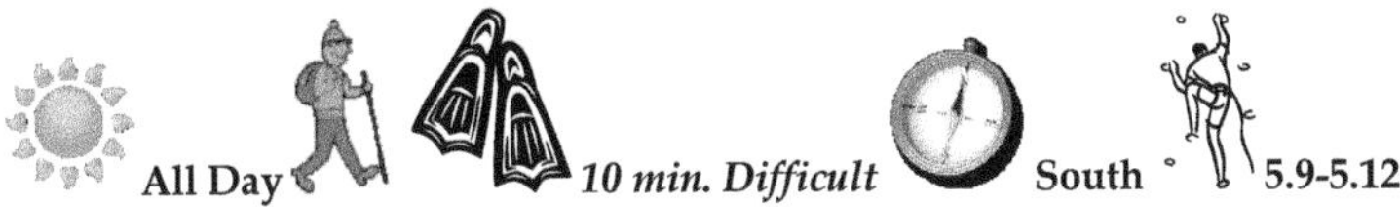


Stunning rock, splitter cracks, and an involved approach characterize this predominantly traditional climbing playground for those seeking old school thrills on intimidating, flaring cracks. Laying low on the river like a sleeping giant, the Indulgence Crag idly waits for the daring climber to scale its difficult walls. With a handful of good moderates, and a slew of hard pitches, *Indulgence* would be a good place to enjoy a day with a proficient climbing partner up for an adventure.

**Approach:** Park on the left side of the road at a small, deep parking spot 40 feet before the double tunnel at 6.9 miles. Walk across the road, down the small scree slope, and follow a well traveled fisherman's trail downriver 100 yards until you can cross a large, wide, shallow part of the river aiming for boulders and the slabs on the left side of the cliff.

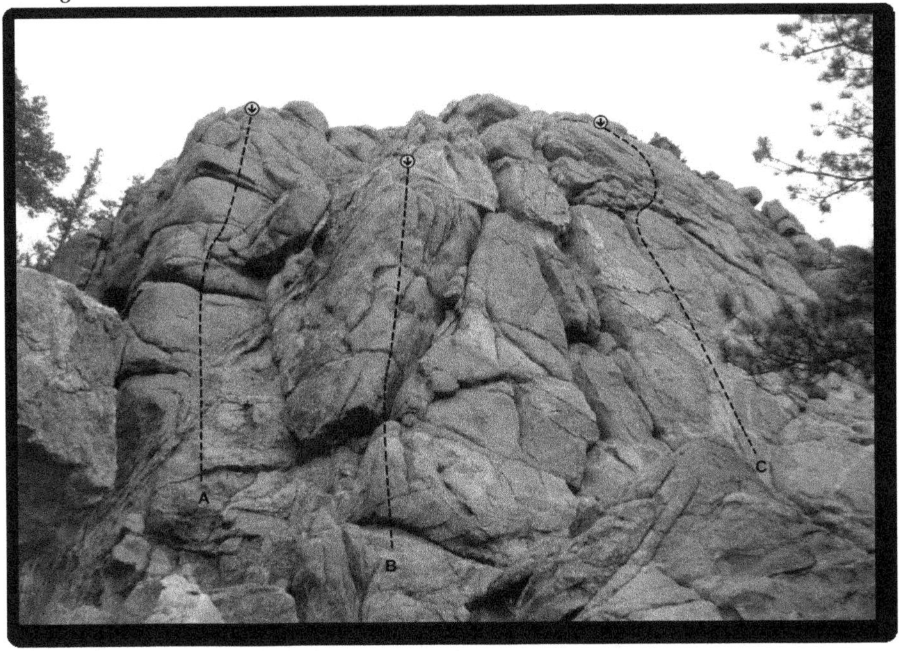

A. **Welcome New Wave** *5.9 ****

On the far left side of the cliff this moderate route takes nice features up the short face to anchors over the lip.
6 bolts. Chain anchor. (50 feet)

B. **Requiem** *5.10a ***

Ten feet to the right of *Welcome New Wave,* this nice line takes the featured arête past easy climbing to a high crux.
4 bolts. Ring Anchor. (40 feet)

C. **The Slinger** *5.9 ****

Brilliant, thin crack climbing up the splitter, finger tip, varnished crack through the slabby, featured panel. Cruxy to start, then sustained with quality gear and marginal rock angling slightly right to high anchors.
Full set of nuts and cams to 1.5". Chain Anchor. (60 feet)
*Bob D'Antonio and Neil Cannon '85*

*60 feet right of the Slinger Panel, and obvious roof with three splitter cracks and large boulders down and right is visible…*

D. **Small Offering** *5.12a **

On the left side of the roof, climb the technical face, five feet right of the right facing dihedral, past a single bolt and multiple flakes to easier ground up broken cracks to summit.

1bolt, medium cams to 2". No anchor. (70 feet)
*Bob D'Antonio and Dale Goddard '85*

E. **The Sanctuary** *5.12c R ***

Climb the left side of the roof above the right angling crack features. Aim for the easiest route to the seam that laterally splits the entire length of the roof. Traverse ten feet right (double ropes might be a good idea!) and then head up the thin seam aiming for a fixed ring piton, through a thin crux to the ledge over and past 30 more feet of 5.5 climbing to the cliff's summit to build a belay. A little flakey, and more of a hassle than it's worth.

1 pin, cams to 3", then small cams and wires through the seam. No anchor. (70 feet)
*Bob D'Antonio and Dale Goddard '85*

F. **The Holding Hand** *5.12b ***

Through the middle of the roof, start up a short hand crack that goes through a small roof (first crux) to gain the juggy ledge that cuts across the entire length of the roof. Traverse 5 feet left (double ropes or long slings might be a good idea!) and climb the right angling crack to the right of an orphan bolt with a rotten white sling. Head up the flaring seam, right over the bulge to low-angle ground to belay on the summit.

Cams and nuts to 3". No anchor. (70 feet)
*Bob D'Antonio and Dale Goddard '85*

*Head up right through a small scramble over the boulders to gain a small hanging plateau 80 feet right of The Holding Hand....*

G. **Catholic Girls** *5.11b ***

On the left side of the alcove, take the flaring slab crack up and left, to a crux switching cracks at ¾ height (the original route ends here) and build a belay under the roof. A better variation takes the crack above the roof to easier climbing up incipient cracks to the summit. Technical, awkward, and flaring.

Cams and nuts to 3". No anchor. (90 feet)
*Bob D'Antonio and Dale Goddard '85*

**H.** **Way Stoned and Snarling** *5.11c* ***

On the right side of the panel take the thin, sustained seam up the overhanging, left facing dihedral past bad feet, decent gear, and an under-cling crux over the roofs past easier climbing to the summit.
Cams and nuts to 3″. Tree anchor. (85 feet)
*Bob D'Antonio and Dale Goddard '85*

**I.** **The Vatican** *5.12b* ****

The area classic! On the panel on the right of the alcove, behind a large pine tree, *The Vatican* takes the beautiful sustained finger crack past a thin, pin protected crux at 30 feet. Then climb a much easier hand crack that angles up left to the summit to build anchors.
Cams and nuts to 1.5″. No anchor. (80 feet)
*Bob D'Antonio and Dale Goddard '85*

*100 feet right of the alcove, scrambling down and right over a death inviting traverse, there is a large, prominent amphitheatre which hosts three good climbs…*

**J.** **Tree Beard** *5.10c* ***

Sustained, quality climbing over a low roof crux to a superb splitter crack on bullet rock. Shared sling anchors with *Crimes of Fashion.*

Double set of cams to 5". Sling anchor. (80 feet)

*Kevin Murray and Steve Cheyney '85*

**K.** **Crimes of Fashion** *5.12b* **

Sketchy climbing over flaky rock in the water streak. Take the left angling crack 15 feet right of *Tree Beard.* Tricky, thin gear over sustained under-clinging and a stemming crux leads up and left to join *Tree Beard's* anchors.

3 pins, fixed nut, and medium to small nuts and cams to 1.5". Rotten sling anchor. (85 feet)

*Mark Rolofson and Bob D'Antonio '82*

**L.** **The Whim** *5.11d R***

Fifteen feet right of *Crimes of Fashion,* take the thin set of finger cracks up gradually lower angling rock up and left using tricky gear. Bad fall potential.

Cams and nuts to 1.5".No anchor.(90 feet)

*Bob D'Antonio and Dale Goddard '84*

*Around the corner to the right of the alcove, bush whack through thorn bushes to the base of the next route…*

**M.** **Indulgence** *5.10b* **

Take the obvious splitter up the south face of the buttress on the right side of the amphitheatre. This route is best broken up into two short pitches. No Topo.

**Pitch 1:** (5.8) Right of the tree, take the splitter cracks to build a belay on the small ledge mid route. Cams and nuts to 3".
No anchor. (40 feet)

**Pitch 2:** (5.10b) Take the splitter hand crack through the face to build an anchor over the summit of the cliff. No Anchor. (40 feet)
Cams and nuts to 3". (80 total feet)

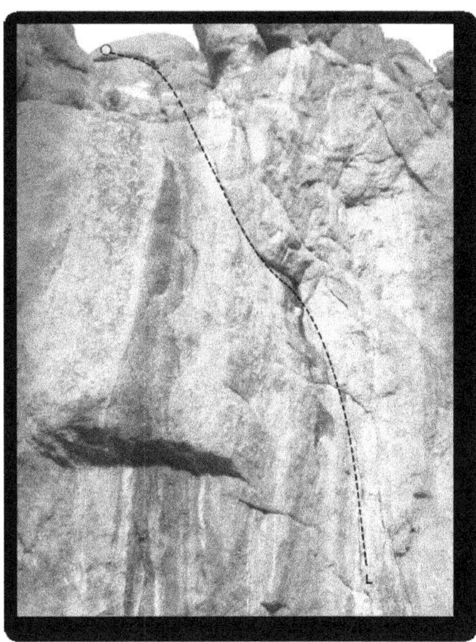

# The River Bloc

*[Hidden in the trees below the west facing, orange streaked wall across the river at 7.3 miles…]*

Amidst a sea of boulders on the wild and adventurous hillside, the River Bloc is a hidden gem of gorgeous water sculpted stone discovered by Bob D'Antonio in 2005. With a rugged, long approach and a handful of decent routes, the boulder is well worth a visit for those who want separation from the crowds that usually overwhelm the more popular crags in Elevenmile.

**Approach:** Park .8 miles beyond the crag at the Cove Campground (and Cove Rock crag). Then walk around the backside of Cove Rock along the north side of the river, past *Genetic Imbalance.* Continue another four hundred yards down the fishing trail to the small valley which hosts the boulder. Another alternative approach is to park at any available pullout near the crag, and scramble down the hillside and wade the river. This is NOT recommended due to the numerous rapids. Use the overhanging, west facing wall on the hillside as a landmark for the crag below.

*Routes are listed from left to right…*

**A.** **Boulder Bottom Feeders** *5.10c* ***

On the left side of the arête of the boulder, take incipient seams up and left past a technical crux to easier climbing on quality stone to anchors.
7 bolts. Ring anchors. (50 feet)
*Bob D'Antonio*

**B.** **Dry Lightning** *5.10b* **

Share the first bolt with *Boulder Bottom Feeders* or climb the thin finger crack on the right side of the arête (small cams to 1"), and climb the arête though many cool positions to shared anchors with *Bottom Feeders.*
5 bolts. Ring anchors. (50 feet)
*Bob D'Antonio*

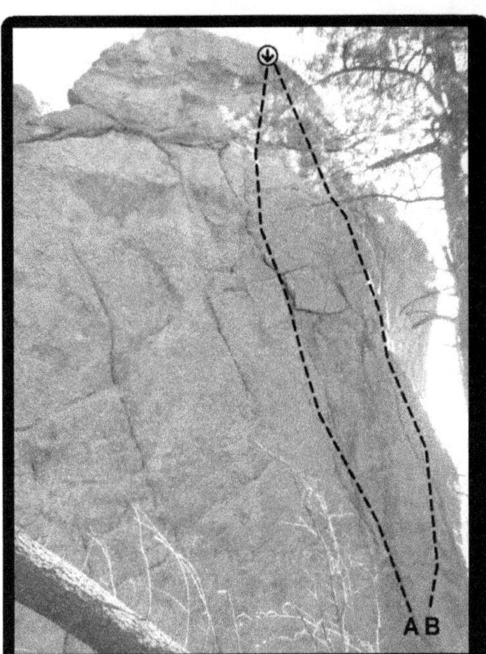


*On the right side of the arête…*

**C.** **Ghost of Tom Joad** 5.11c **

Climb the beautiful, left trending hand crack to the bolt protected, face moves over the lip. Nice mixed route!

3 bolts, medium cams to 3". No anchors. (50 feet)

*Bob D'Antonio*

**D.** **Kid Smoke** 5.12a **

On the right side of the boulder, take scoop features past orange bolts up and right over the lip. Varied, technical face climbing!

5 bolts. Ring anchors. (50 feet)

*Bob D'Antonio*

# Cove Rock

*[Located across the river on the east side of Cove Campground at 7.7 miles]*

Sitting casually next to the river, catching the rays of the western sun, which warm the cliff to perfect climbing temperature in the fall months, Cove rock offers 4 decent routes. Among them being the uber classic *Breakfast in America,* which is arguably the canyon's best splitter crack up the right side the face.

**Approach:** Park at the large pullout directly across from the crag, and walk upstream to the Cove Rock Campground entrance. Make your way down the road, past the campsites to the cliff.

**A.** **Chicago Blues** *5.11c* *
A hard start on sloping, technical climbing leads to steeper terrain with a crux over a small roof. Keep it together for the face above! Worthwhile and generously bolted!
5 bolts. Cold-shut anchors. (40 feet)
*Bob D'Antonio and Chuck Carlson '94*

**B.** **Neither Wolf Nor Dog** *5.12b* **
A hard technical start on slopers and crimps through slightly chossy rock, leads to the pumpy, overhanging roof crack above. A varied climb that is protected well!
4 bolts and a #2 cam. Cold-shut anchors. (50 feet)
*Bob D'Antonio and Chuck Carlson*

C. **Breakfast in America** *5.11b* ****

Utterly classic finger crack! Start in the small overhanging cave, make powerful moves with good protection to a rest above the lip. From here its sustained action packed tip jamming, with a crux throw at the top of the crack to a bomber jug! Awesome climbing with great pro characterize this must do route!
Small to medium nuts and cams, multiple finger sizes. Rap anchors. (40 feet)
*Bob D'Antonio '81*

D. **Savage Grace** *5.11d R* *

You'd better be on your "A" game for this one. Hard, technical, and dangerous climbing lead to the first bolt. After that, the climbing backs off a little to get over the bulge, which leads to a mantle over the ledge. Build a station over the lip.
Small stoppers, cams, and RP's. No anchor. (40 feet)
*Bob D'Antonio and Will Gadd '84*

*300 yards downstream of Cove Rock behind the formation lies a large boulder with a single route. Walk up over the hill past the left side of Cove Rock. Walk down the fisherman's trail that parallels the river, passing a sign that says "Danger: Rapids Ahead, Floating Not Recommended," and continue down the trail until you reach a large, south facing boulder with a crack up the middle, protected by bolts…*

E. **Genetic Imbalance** *5.12a* **

A short and powerful crack climb! Start with powerful lie-backing up a finger flake past two SMC hangers to a crux transition up and left. Supplement this section with a finger sized cam, and follow the crack up and left to clip a pin and go over the roof. Cool setting next to the river!
2 bolts and one pin, and a finger sized cam. No Anchor. (30 feet)
*Bob D'Antonio and Richard Aschert '85*

# The Icebox

*[Located on the south side of the road at 7.9 miles, before the bridge]*

The Icebox is an immaculate cliff. Gorgeous rock, lush foliage, and close proximity to the car make this crag a very an enjoyable place to spend warm afternoons, or catch a break from the summer sun. This steep, west-facing crag has been looked at for a long time, but it wasn't until local activists Bob D'Antonio, Ian and Stewart Green, Bill Schmausser, and Kelly Baldwin began development in 2005 that the prime new routes were established. In recent years, local hard man Chris Barlow contributed a handful of harder routes, notably his *Sub Zero* (5.13a) which claims the throne as Elevenmile's hardest traditional route. Thanks to the efforts of these individuals, this serene crag offers incredible variety and many of Elevenmile's best climbs, and is the first place you should stop when you have climbers with varied abilities in your group.

**Approach:** Park just before the bridge at one of the two pullouts at 7.9 miles. Take the trail through the bushes, and the long cliff band will be just on your left.

A. **Ice, Ice Baby** *5.12b* **

The leftmost line of bolts on the cliff, stem your way up a shallow right facing dihedral to a vertical slab crux, then plug in gear through the thin hand crack (red point crux) over the roof.

6 bolts, small cams to 2". Ring anchors. (45 feet)

*Bob D'Antonio '05*

B. **Friction Fix** *5.11c* ***

A mixed route, this varied climb starts just right of the small cave. Using both crack and sport skills, work your way through a slab crux at the second bolt (with decking potential without the small cam) to steep climbing up high. A varied adventure!

8 bolts. Small to medium nuts and cams. Rappel anchors. (80 feet)

*Bob D'Antonio and Kelly Baldwin '04*

C. **Rodeo Clowns** *5.12a* **

Take the right bolted line of the small cave, and edge your way past multiple thin cruxes and lock-offs past a handful of rests to join the anchors of *Friction Fix.*

7 bolts. Ring anchors. (80 feet)

*Kelly Baldwin and Bob D'Antonio*

D. **Ice on the Moon** *5.11c* **

The left of the two routes on this panel, this line takes easy climbing up the slab to a thin, brief, roof crux. Head up right via sustained edging to anchors.

7 bolts. Ring anchors. (90 feet)

*Kelly Baldwin and Bob D'Antonio*

E. **Disney on Ice** *5.11b* ***

Start 15 feet right of *Ice on the Moon*. Fun slab moves past three bolts deposit you below the overhang. Mount, grovel, or finesse your way over the "Whales Tail" crux, and do a couple more balancy, slab moves to the anchor. As with many routes on this wall, this one requires a diversity of climbing skills!

9 bolts. Chain anchors. (90 feet)

*Kelly Baldwin '04*

F. **Ice Cube** *5.11b* **

Forty feet to the right of *Disney on Ice,* this route takes a technical, bolt protected slab crux to join a long flake leading to a roof. This section can be supplemented with gear, and should be, as pulling the cruxy roof leads to a sustained slab above. No topo.

6 bolts, midsized cams to 3". Ring anchors. (70 feet)

*Kelly Baldwin and Bob D'Antonio*

*50 feet uphill from the lower collection of sport routes, the next collection of stellar lines begins on a small plateau to the right of a very large pine tree…*

G. **Trads Are People Too** *5.9* ***

Starting below an obvious right facing corner 10 feet left of *Queen Byron*, take the stellar corner up and over the roof crux to a technical sport protected section to anchors at a break. Nice climbing!

Cams and nuts to 3", 3 bolts. Ring anchor. (75 feet)

*Bill Schmausser*

H. **Queen Byron** *5.11c* ***

Named after a hardcore Springs local who had a particularly feminine look during a photo shoot, this quality route shouldn't be missed. Edge and pull up a beautiful, sharp arête to a thin, crimp crux at the roof. Pull up and right past easier climbing to a small dihedral and finish at anchors.

7 bolts. Chain anchor. (50 feet)

*Bill Schmausser*

I. **Bob the Roofer** *5.11d* **

Interesting mixed climb over good rock. Start just left of *Hemisphere* on, small boulders and make your way up an easy dihedral crack to a roof. Clip a bolt, and pull the roof up and left past two more bolts to finish on the anchors of *Queen Byron.* The crux is short lived and hard.

3 bolts, cams to 2". Chain anchor. (50 feet)

*Bob D' Antonio '04*

J. **Hemisphere** *5.10a* ****

Fun climbing through under-clings and knobs up a right trending slab. When the angle begins to get steep there lies a powerful, technical arête crux. Finish with a fun pull over the lip to anchors. Well protected and good position.

7 bolts. Chain Anchors. (55 feet)

*Bill Schmausser*

K. **Corneal Abrasion** *5.6* ****

An outstanding climb for beginners and kids. Interesting, well protected, slab moves over great stone, make this one of the best of its grade in the canyon. You can walk to the top of the ledge 60 feet up for a quick top rope.

7 bolts. Ring anchors. (45 feet)

*Bill Schamausser '05*

L. **Brain Freeze** *5.10d* ****

Don't miss this route!!!! Great movement on excellent stone! Start by climbing *Corneal Abrasion.* Either belay here, or link it into the next section, which starts with juggy steep moves aiming for the crack. Stem, technique, and body jam your way up the right side of the big off-width, then cut right up to the anchors. If you link this, you **must use a 70 meter rope!**

15 bolts. Ring Anchors. (120 feet)

*Bob D'Antonio '05*

*The next set of routes are accessed by walking right up the hill, then cutting back left through the pine trees which open up to a large alcove 50 feet up from the slabs below. The first route on the far left ledge is...*

M. **The Micro Fridge** *5.12b* ***

Starting off the ledge up and right of *Brain Freeze* (scramble up and right around the cliff and traverse back left to the base of the route). Start by lie-backing seams, and making powerful moves up a right leaning seam. A boulder crux hits at the bulge, which requires a long move, then fire up a "tufa" to the anchors. Excellent powerful climbing up one of the coolest features in the icebox!

7 bolts. Lower offs. (70 feet)

*Chris Barlow '09*

N. **10th Ave. Freeze Out** *5.11c* ***

The first route on the steep section of rock, this route tackles the prominent, fin riddled arête. The crux hits right off the deck (a recommended stick clip for the first bolt), and follows juggy overhanging terrain to a scenic anchor. Physical climbing!

6 bolts. Three Ring anchors. (60 feet)
*Bob D'Antonio '05*

O. **Ice Age** *5.11b* **

Take the first crux boulder problem (a stick clip is a good idea) up and right, aiming for a large, right facing dihedral. Stem your way up this feature then cut back left to shared anchors with *Tenth Avenue.*

7 bolts. Three Ring anchors. (60 feet)
*Bob D'Antonio '05*

P. **Funkalicious** *5.12d* **

Where the cliff begins to get really steep, this bouldery route hits you right off the deck with action packed moves! The crux involves bear hugging a huge block, but keep it together for the steep finish to the good ledge. Multiple cruxes with a few chances to rest along the way, recommended!

7 bolts. Lower off anchors. (75 feet)
*Ian-Spencer Green '06*

Q.  **Project** *5.13*

A new Barlow mixed route taking the first two bolts of the *Ice Boxer* and then cutting up left to join broken seams to chain anchors directly between those of *Funkalicious* and *Ice Boxer.*

2 bolts, cams and nuts to 3". (80 feet)
*Chris Barlow '10*

R.  **The Ice Boxer** *5.13c* ****

This proud line takes the path of least resistance up the main part of the overhanging face. Boulder up the first 2 bolts, then cut right to a juggy rest. From here it's pumpy, technical, lie-backing moves through multiple cruxes, to the heartbreakingly thin crux that guards the anchors. Soft in the grade, this is recommended, pumpy endurance climbing!

10 bolts. Lower off anchors. (80 feet)
*Ian-Spencer Green '06*

**S.** **Sub-Zero** *5.13a* **

Powerful, sloping, and dynamic! Start by stick clipping the first black bolt and stem your way past chossy rock to a rest below the bulge. From here it's on, placing small (but good) gear in thin cracks and hard bouldering all the way to the chains! Elevenmile's hardest crack!

Cams to 2", 2 bolts. Chain anchor. (45 feet)

*Chris Barlow '10*

*40 feet up hill from sub zero, scramble up the steep trail (which is usually either frozen or a stream) to the alcove where the last three routes lie…*

**T.** **Frozen In Time** *5.12a* ****

This great route takes the prominent line up the arête on the very right side of the Icebox, on the left side of the far right alcove. Start with technical moves up the steep slab, then fire through bigger holds to a crux below the anchor on the face up and left. Steep, pumpy climbing on slightly chossy rock with great cruxes. A great route for the aspiring 5.12 climber!

8 bolts. Lower off anchor. (50 feet)

*Brian Shelton and Bob D' Antonio '06*

**U.** **Landscape Architect** *5.10c* ***

Great climbing on some of Elevenmile's best stone! Climb up easy jugs to a ledge. Then stem, grovel, or finesse your way up the bulging, crack feature crux to an easier slab above.

8 bolts. Chain anchor. (45 feet)

*Bill Schmausser*

**V.** **A Hard Rain's Gonna Fall** *5.10b* **

Easy looking climbing on the far right side of the cliff past a low, powerful crux over large sloping jugs leads to casual climbing above. Deceptive and colder than the rest of the routes here.

7 Bolts. Cold-shut Anchor. (45 feet)

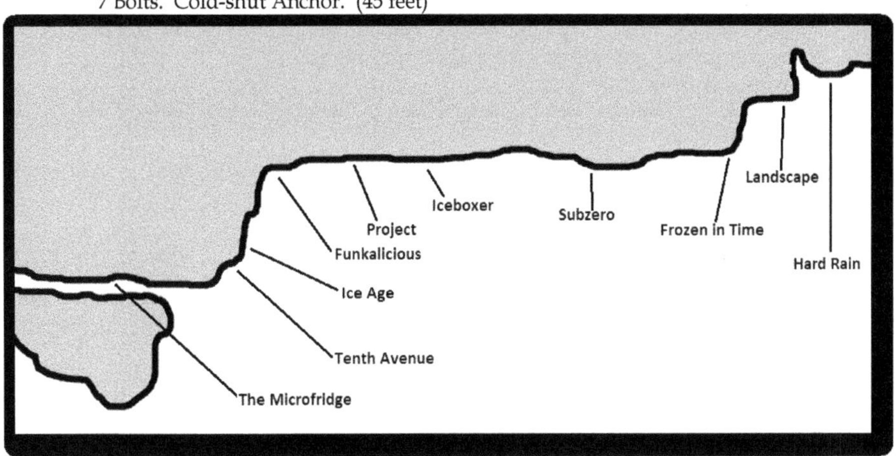

# Pine Cone Dome

*[Located adjacent to the road at 8.0 miles]*

Imagine a gorgeous, bullet hard, 150 foot tall cliff that's 2 minutes from the road. Now picture a smorgasbord of three and four star routes from 5.5 to 5.12, where you can climb in the winter months, and is graced by a beautiful aspen grove that blankets the valley floor below. This dream cliff is real, and accounts for its popularity for the past 20 years. With new additions of many classic sport pitches, every climber will surely find something entertaining at this crag!

**Approach:** Park at any of the pullouts on the road opposite the cliff, and find one of the numerous well traveled climber's trails that lead to the wall.

*Approach the following three routes from the Idlewild Picnic area parking…*

**A.** **Pine Nuts** *5.7 R* *

Decent climbing, but very difficult to protect as the pro is sparse. Take a flaring flake up and right to an obvious dihedral. Used as an approach pitch to create its neighbor *Conarrete,* and shares anchors with the first pitch of that route.
Small nuts and cams to 1". Chain anchor. (80 feet)
*Paul Obanhein and Peggy Evleth '10*

**B.** **Conarette** ***5.10d*** ***

**Pitch 1** (5.10d): Takes the prominent arête through a crux at the face up to a large ledge. The crux is brief and well protected. Quality climbing!
8 bolts. Bolt anchor. (80 feet)
**Pitch 2** (5.8): Takes the face up and right to an anchor at the summit of the cliff.
4 bolts. Bolt anchor. (70 feet)
10 bolts. Bolt anchors. (150 total feet)
*Paul Obanhein and Peggy Evleth '10*

**C.** **Pathogen** *5.11* *

Nice technical arête climbing over interesting features to a blank crux where a huge jug broke off. Approach this route from the parking area at Idlewild, as getting through the sticker bushes is very unpleasant!
4 bolts. Chain anchors. (35 feet)
*Bill Schmausser*

A
B
C
D

*The following pitch is located in the boulders below the Pine Cone Dome proper…*

**D.**  **Stemulation** *5.10b* **

Start in the obvious dihedral between the big boulders below the Dome. Make a couple of difficult flaring moves through a crux down low, then clip a bolt and angle up right under a small roof to clip the anchors.
Cams to 3". Bolt anchor. (40 feet)

*On the left side of the dome proper, it's better to access these routes by walking up from the various pullouts below the main dome…*

**E.**  **Toy Cows in Africa** *5.10c* ****

Fantastic climbing! This is a great outing over good rock and nice position on the left side of the Dome. Pitches 1 and 2 can be linked for an awesome long climb.
**Pitch 1**(5.9): Start up a technical slab and angle left up good rock through interesting water pods and crimps with good protection to chain anchors.
Chain Anchors. (50 feet)
**Pitch 2** (5.10c): Climb up and left to an engaging, crimpy crux a past couple bolts off of the belay, follow intricate and enjoyable climbing up to anchors at the very top of the Dome! This route is one of the top ten, and one of the best 5.10's in the canyon. Use One rope to get off in two raps, or **you must use a 70m rope for a single rap**!
Chain Anchors. (55 feet)
25 bolts. Two chain anchor Belays. (130 feet)
*Bill Schmausser*

**F.**  **Neck Row Feel Ya** *5.10c*

This route is run-out and dangerous over sections of suspect rock. There is a reason this has become overgrown and unpopular. Crux is a pull over the roof at 2/3 height, then it's run-outs of death from there.
Nuts and cams to a #3 camalot. No Anchor. (100 feet)

**G.**  **Anorexic Lycra Dog** *5.12a* ***

One of Elevenmile's most enjoyable, difficult slab climbs. A good hard lead on excellent holds! Start just left of the *Roof Bypass* crack, and take the prominent line of bolts up the slab to finish below the roof to a ridiculously wide bolted belay.
6 bolts. Rappel Anchors. (50 feet)
*Brian Mullins Charles Walter*

E
F
G
H
I
J
K
L
M
N
O
P
Q
R
S

H. **Roof Bypass** *5.7+* ****

The best traditional route on the Dome, which is beautiful, sustained, and brilliant! Both pitches can be linked with a 60m rope, but many people just break it up.
**Pitch 1:** (5.7+): Take the super obvious right facing dihedral through continuous and sustained climbing to a high crux. Belay up and right of the left roof 15 feet up on a good ledge out right. If there is no one on *Talk to Your Toes,* that anchor is a good alternative to building one. Ultra classic!
Nuts and Cams to 3", with a couple to 5". No anchor. (70 feet)
**Pitch 2:** (5.5) Continue above the belay ledge following well protected, moderate climbing to belay at a tree on the summit. Cams and nuts to 3". Tree anchor. (70 feet)
Full set of cams and nuts to 3", with a couple to 5". (140 total feet)

I. **Talk to Your Toes** *5.10a* ***

To the right of *Roof Bypass* this new sport route takes the technical slab past a crux getting to the first bolt, then follow easier, sustained climbing to the anchors. A nice addition!
6 bolts. Rappel anchor. (70 feet)
*Paul Obanhein, Clay Sanford, and Janice Sakata '10*

J. **Blossoming Bosoms** *5.9* **

**Pitch 1:** (5.8): Take the crack and seam between the two bolted lines up right of the bolted station, past some dicey run-outs to build a belay at the intersection of *Roof Bypass* 30 feet above its first pitch.
Nuts and Cams to 3". No anchor. (100 feet)
**Pitch 2:** (5.7) Continue above the belay ledge angling right to a thin crack with good protection, to finish up and left below the small roof which leads to much easier climbing to the summit. Cams and nuts to 3". Tree anchor. (55 feet)
Cams and nuts to 3". Tree anchor. (155 total feet)

K. **New Sport** *5.10b* ***

Take the line of shiny bolts to the right of *Blossoming Bosoms* and cross over that route to join the anchors of *Talk to Your Toes* after a high crux. Good fun!
8 bolts. Rappel Anchor. (75 feet)

L. **Lichen or Leave It** *5.9* **

**Pitch 1:** (5.8): Take the obvious dihedral left of the bolted sport routes through easy 5.6 climbing for most of the way to a short section of 5.8 hand crack in the left facing corner. Belay at the good belay ledge just above this section.
Nuts and Cams to 3", with a couple to 6". No anchor. (55 feet)
**Pitch 2:** (5.7) Continue above the belay ledge angling right to a thin crack with good protection, to finish up and left below the small roof which yields much easier climbing to the summit. Cams and nuts to 3". Tree anchor. (85 feet)
Cams and nuts to 3". Tree anchor. (140 total feet)

M. **Ben Dover** *5.9+* ***

Forty feet right of *Roof Bypass* , this line takes the left side of the clean panel. Popular, wandering, and interesting; this was one of the first modern sport routes in the canyon. The pun indicates the sandbagged nature of the route, and the bolting may feel a bit old school.

6 bolts. Chain anchor. (55 feet)

*Brian Mullin*

N. **Curt Loves Ugly** *5.11b* ***

Take the technical panel past two bolts to a reachy crux. Take advantage of the rest, as it's a cruise up sustained but easier edging to shared anchors with *Ben Dover*.

5 bolts. Ring Anchor. (55 feet)

*Bob D'Antonio '05*

O. **Bye, Bye Butterfly** *5.11c* ***

One of the better 5.11's at the crag, this sustained and continuous crimp and slab fest never lets up! Start on slabby, left trending jugs and begin the long road of high steps, crimps, and delicate friction moves which lead to the infamous "crystal" crux. The route may feel easier if you're tall!

8 bolts. Chain anchors. (60 feet)

*Bob D'Antonio '05*

P. **To Bubb or Not to Be** *5.9+* **

**Pitch 1:** (5.9) Ten feet to the right of *Bye Bye Butterfly,* climb the small dihedral crack through multiple technical cruxes to build a belay on the ledge 15 feet left of *Kayak's* anchors.

Cams and nuts to 3". No anchor. (55 feet)

**Pitch 2:** (5.7) Continue above the belay ledge through a vegetated crack on the left side of a panel, getting good gear up the broken face to belay at a tree at the summit. Cams and nuts to 3". No anchor. (85 feet)

Cams and nuts to 3". Tree anchor. (140 total feet)

*Bob D'Antonio '05*

Q. **Kayak for Sale** *5.10d* ****

Fantastic climbing on nice, beautiful, black rock! Climb up an easy left trending flake, then angle up right through a long, thin, and technical crux that is well protected. Finish through run-out but good holds up to anchors over the lip.

8 bolts. Chain anchor. (60 feet)

*Bob D'Antonio*

**R.** **Stone Age** *5.6* **

A decent, popular, moderate pitch up very nice features, it will not be uncommon to wait in line for this one.

**Pitch 1** (5.6): In the deep, obvious dihedral 30 feet right of *Kayak,* stem your way up placing large gear to clip a pin at 25 feet, then continue up easier ground to the tree anchor which is shared by the following two routes. This makes for a good long pitch using a 60m rope. Large cams and nuts to 5″. Tree anchor. (120 feet)

**Pitch 2** (5.3): Angle up and right to the summit over easy terrain (any path will do) to walk off the back. Small cams and nuts to 2″. Tree anchor. (60 feet)

Full rack of cams and nuts to 5″. (180 total feet)

**S.** **Armaj Das** *5.6* **

A decent moderate pitch which serves for those comfortable with 5.7 traditional climbing.

**Pitch 1** (5.6): Fifteen feet to the right of the large dihedral on the far left of the panel, and take a vague system of flakes between ledges past a pin at 15 feet, and follow gradually easier climbing up to the tree to build a belay. This makes for a good, long pitch using a 60m rope. Large cams and nuts to 4″. Tree anchor. (120 feet)

**Pitch 2** (5.3): Angle up and right to summit over easy terrain (any path will do) to walk off the back.

Small cams and nuts to 2″. Tree anchor. (60 feet)

**T.** **She's a Moaner** *5.9+ ****

A long run-out to the first bolt gives way to easier climbing with a crux above the 5th bolt. Named for the sounds made by a first ascentionist who was very involved with her effort on the route. Interesting moves!
5 bolts. Chain anchor. (70 feet)
*Bob D'Antonio and Kelly Baldwin '04*

**U.** **Don't Go** *5.9 ***

The middle route on the panel. Start with a steep, bolt protected crux over slopers and crimps, which leads to jugs in a cracks and continues to anchors over the lip. A nice bolt and gear lead!
2 bolts, medium cams and nuts to 3″. Chain anchors. (55 feet)
*Bob D'Antonio and Kelly Baldwin '04*

**V.** **Balancing Act** *5.10c ***

Start on the steep slab just left of *Jolly Jugular*, and make tenuous and scary moves to a crux after the second bolt. After that the climbing backs off significantly, giving way to long run-outs past jugs (bolts 4 and 5) up and left to shared anchors. A decent route with odd bolt placements, this should be re-engineered.
6 bolts. Chain anchors. (55 feet)

**W.** **Jolly Jugular** *5.5 ****

A fine, moderate pitch, which serves as a good introduction to trad climbing. A 5.8 variation called *Halo Addiction* was chopped but can be top-roped off of the anchors from this route.
**Pitch 1** (5.5): Starting just left of the *Punks* face, climb up the obvious dihedral, which consists of jugs and bomber gear placements, and follow it to a small roof where the angle backs off significantly. Cut up and left from here, aiming for a tree and a large ledge to build a belay. Large cams and nuts to 4″. Tree anchor. (120 feet)
**Pitch 2** (5.3): Angle up and right to the summit over easy terrain to walk off the back. Small cams and nuts to 2″. Tree anchor. (60 feet)

**X.** **Punks and Old Men** *5.8 *****

One of the best, easy climbs on the Dome! Well protected with a crux down low, to easier slab moves toward the anchors. May seem a little stout for the grade, but this route is well worth doing!
7 bolts. Chain anchors. (50 feet)
*Bill Schmausser '05*

**Y.** **Parr Four** *5.10b **

A contrived and wandering choss pile.
**Pitch 1** (5.9): Starting 10 feet right of *Punks,* climb the shallow dihedral up loose and dirty climbing to build a belay at a right facing block, up left below a right curving splitter crack. Cams and nuts to 4″. No anchor. (90 feet)
**Pitch 2** (5.10b): The only redeemable part of this route, take the right curving, splitter crack up to join the obvious right facing dihedral of *Squid Face.* Finish up that route. Cams and nuts to 3″. Tree anchor. (80 feet)
Full rack of cams and nuts to 3″. (170 total feet)

**Z.** **Squid Face** *5.9+*

Poor gear, grungy crack, loose rock, and contrived. Start on the slabs and short corners making 5.8 moves, aiming for a right facing dihedral. Crux moves lead into a corner, then follow it to the top of the cliff and walk off the back side.
Cams and nuts to 3". No anchor. (190 feet)
*Brent Kertzman and Dave Brower '86*

**A.** **Open Project** *5.13* **

On the vast slab left of *Harder than it Looks,* take an easy 5.4 hand crack up to join 5 bolts through the horizontal slabs. Difficult smearing to a blank section before the roof where a huge flake broke off.
5 bolts, small to medium cams. No Anchor. (100 feet)
*Bill Schmausser*

**B.** **Harder Than It Looks** *5.10a* **

Fun but difficult climbing over good rock, past 3 bolts leads to a technical, left trending crux out under-clings in a roof. Finish up an easy crack (place a piece or two) to anchors at the break. Looks like 5.7, but climbs like 5.10!
4 bolts, and a .75 Camalot. Chain anchors. (45 feet)

**C.** **Stories for Boys** *5.11a* ***

An interesting mixed route that was accidentally re-bolted, but reflects the open mind of the first ascentionist when he says, "I like the new variation better." Slabby start off a boulder leads to a big dihedral, where it switches from bolts to gear. Climb up to a crux roof where the bolts re-appear. Finish with a nice slab to anchors.
5 bolts, and three cams (0.4, 0.5, 0.75). Chain anchors. (75 feet)
*Bob D'Antonio and Bill Schmausser*

D. **Wrestle With the Pig** *5.9* **

On the far right side of the Dome in an aspen grove, this adventurous climb takes interesting features over a crux roof, with a slabby red-point crux over the lip. Some have called this classic, others have said it's a miserable choss pile, but it's adventurous in any respect!

9 bolts. Chain anchors. (75 feet)

*Bob D'Antonio*

# Idlewild

*[Located on the north side of the road by Idlewild Picnic area at 8.1 miles]*

This varied and complex labyrinth of climbs and boulders is by far the most convoluted and tricky to navigate climbing in Elevenmile Canyon. Most of the routes here are short, steep, hard, and old school, which is why they haven't gained much popularity over the years. Bob D' Anotonio, Mark Milligan, and Brent Kertzmen were the main developers of the crag, testing their skills through various solos and difficult mixed climbs that scale the steeper canyon faces. For those willing to make the effort, the handful of test pieces (as well as a few new mixed routes) should keep the proficient climber occupied for a day or two.

**Approach:** Park at the picnic area, and take any of the various forks via social trails to reach your desired route.

*The following routes are in the west fork of the canyon, accessed by walking left up a picnicker's trail which begins where the rocks narrow, 40 feet north of the Idlewild bathroom. On the west side of the canyon…*

A. **Dale Solo** *5.10c* *

The first route on the left. Begin in front of an aspen tree and climb the right trending, exfoliating crack which cuts back left through a crux finish to top out the crag. Nuts and cams to 3". No anchor. (30 feet)

*Dale Goddard and Bob D'Antonio '84*

*30 feet up from Dale…*

B. **Rubber Soul** *5.12a* *

Sustained face climbing up frequently wet and exfoliating rock to a crux at 2/3 height. Frequently the home of multiple bail biners, which indicate the quality of the pitch.

4 bolts. Single bolt anchor. (40 feet)

*Bob D'Antonio and Chuck Carlson '94*

C. **Escape From Alabama** *5.11d* *

Ten feet right of *Rubber*, take the line up a tiny corner to clip a high bolt, then crux it up past one more hidden bolt to join a thin crack leading up over the lip. Decent rock up high but the protection is old and dangerous.

One bolt, nuts and cams to 2". No anchor. (50 feet)

*Bob D'Antonio '86*

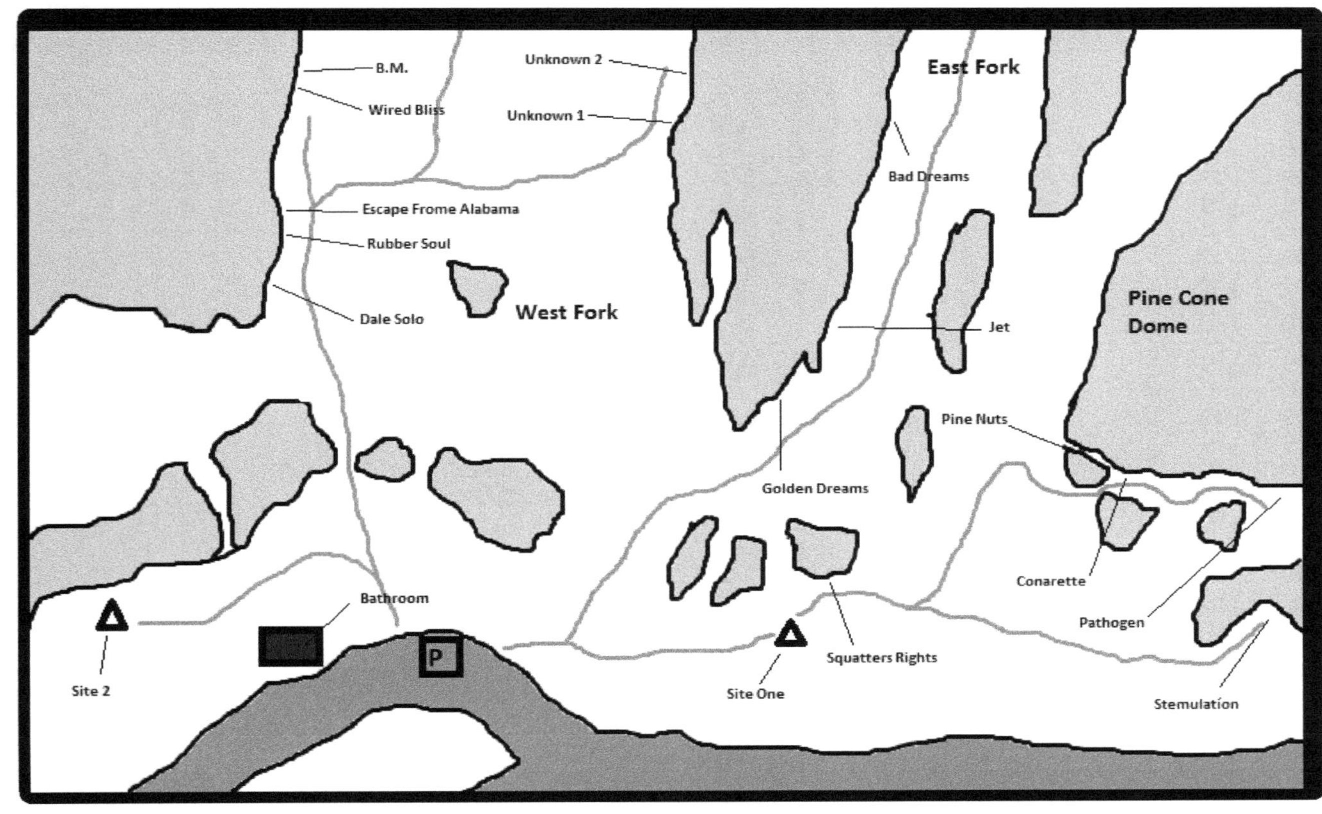
B.M.
Wired Bliss
Unknown 2
Unknown 1
East Fork
Bad Dreams
Escape Frome Alabama
Rubber Soul
Dale Solo
West Fork
Jet
Pine Cone
Dome
Pine Nuts
Golden Dreams
Conarette
Bathroom
P
Pathogen
Site 2
Squatters Rights
Site One
Stemulation

*30 feet right of escape…*

**D.** **Wired Bliss** *5.11d* *

Take the flaring, vegetated hand crack over a small bulge to join a crack system that leads straight up to belay at a ledge.

Nuts and cams to 3". No anchor. (50 feet)

*Bob D'Antonio '84*

**E.** **B.M.** *5.13a*

Five feet right of *Wired* take the right trending, flaring finger crack past a junk, old pin and a bad bolt with no hanger to finish over the lip. A stick clip is recommended (although this route is not!), but probably won't do you much good…utter garbage!

1 bolt, 1 pin. No anchor. (25 feet)

*Bob Murray and Bob D'Antonio '84*

*On the East side of the left fork, routes are listed from right to left…*

**F.** **Unknown One** *5.11a* **

On the right side of a small alcove, take a small slab protected by a single modern bolt to join a finger crack, which leads up and left over the technical slab past many bulges to hidden anchors.

7 bolts, nuts and cams to 2". Ring Anchor. (70 feet)

**G.** **Unknown Two** *5.10b* **

Twenty feet left of *Unknown One*, clip a low bolt and take the juggy, hand and finger crack up and left to nice climbing past four more bolts to anchors.

5 bolts, nuts and cams to 3". Ring Anchor. (70 feet)

*Heading up and right from the crack riddled cliff in the parking area, scramble up through an aspen grove to join the east fork of the canyon…*

**H.** **Golden Dreams** *5.12b* ***

On a gorgeous overhanging panel, climb the ridiculously thin face up and left, past two bolts to join a superb right leaning crack which leads to the summit. A stick clip is recommended to back up the old bolts.

2 bolts, nuts and cams to 3". No Anchor. (50 feet)

*Bob D'Antonio '84*

*Heading right toward the first picnic area, above the table lies…*

**I.** **Squatters Rights** *5.11d* *

Take the unprotected slab up to a short, overhanging finger crack through the small bulge. Finish up easier cracks to anchors.

Nuts and cams to 3". No Anchor. (30 feet)

*Bob D'Antonio '84*

# Camp Rock

*[Located immediately on the north side of the road at 8.3 miles]*

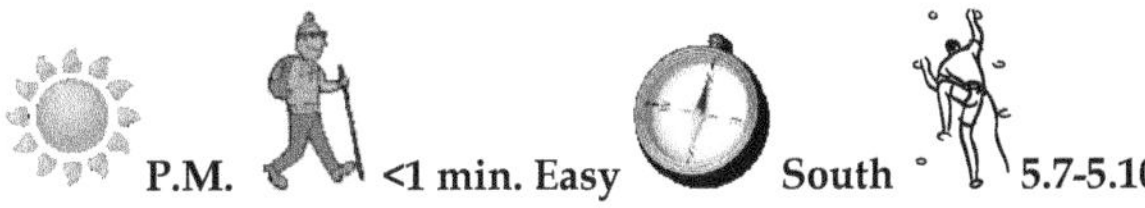


Probably the most summited cliff in Elevenmile. Camp Rock is almost always swarming with campers and eager tourists who walk up the backside of the cliff on hot summer days to get a better view of the river below Spillway Campground. Many climbers only use this crag as a meeting spot to park their cars before heading up to the bigger and better crags, but it still hosts a couple decent, end-of-the-day pitches for those looking for a quick lap. There are many great top roping opportunities on this cliff. While many have been climbed, the FA info has drifted into obscurity.

*On the left side of the crag, above the boulders lies…*

**A.** **Fisherman Watching** *5.10d* *

Start off the boulders and angle right past funky pulls and mantles. Climb past two oddly placed bolts to the crack which leads to the summit. Cool line, weird protection.
2 bolts, nuts and cams to 3". No Anchor. (55 feet)

*30 feet right of Fisherman…*

**B.** **Cave Crack** *5.7* **

Begin in the obvious, wide crack in a right facing dihedral directly in the middle of the cliff. Dodge the thorn bushes, and climb out the "cave" past a low crux and a nice hand and fist crack, to reach easier climbing through the dihedral above. Build an anchor at the lip.
Nuts and cams to 4". No Anchor. (60 feet)

C. **Log Jam** 5.8 **

Ten feet right of *Cave Crack,* take the unprotect-able face past some balancy moves to join the next wide crack system 10 feet right of *Cave Crack.* Climb off the ledge, traversing left to finish up the wide crack through the face paralleling the end of *Cave Crack.*
Nuts and cams to 4". No Anchor. (60 feet)

*30 feet right of Log Jam, on the right side of the cliff…*

D. **The Forgotten** 5.9 *

Take the cool bulbous features past a single bolt, to continuously steeper climbing (and tricky gear placements) over the lip.
Nuts and cams to 2", 1 bolt. No Anchor. (60 feet)

# The Corridor Crags

*[Located on the hiking trail, in the corridor, 300 feet east of Baboon Rock]*

In the hot summer evenings, the corridor crag is a welcome sight after lounging all day at the Spillway Campground, and the hiking trail gives phenominal views of Elevenmile Reservior and the west end of the canyon. The routes here are vague and old school; however, there is decent potentail for those looking to walk in the footsteps of the early developers of Elevenmile.

**Approach:** From the parking area, walk along the road into Spillway Campground for about 100 yards until a large, overhanging boulder is visible on your right. Take the well maintained, obvious hiking trail which leads to the top of Baboon Rock. The trail is well marked and popular, and should be obvious as it leads up and right through a gully and then through a small corridor where the cliff lies.

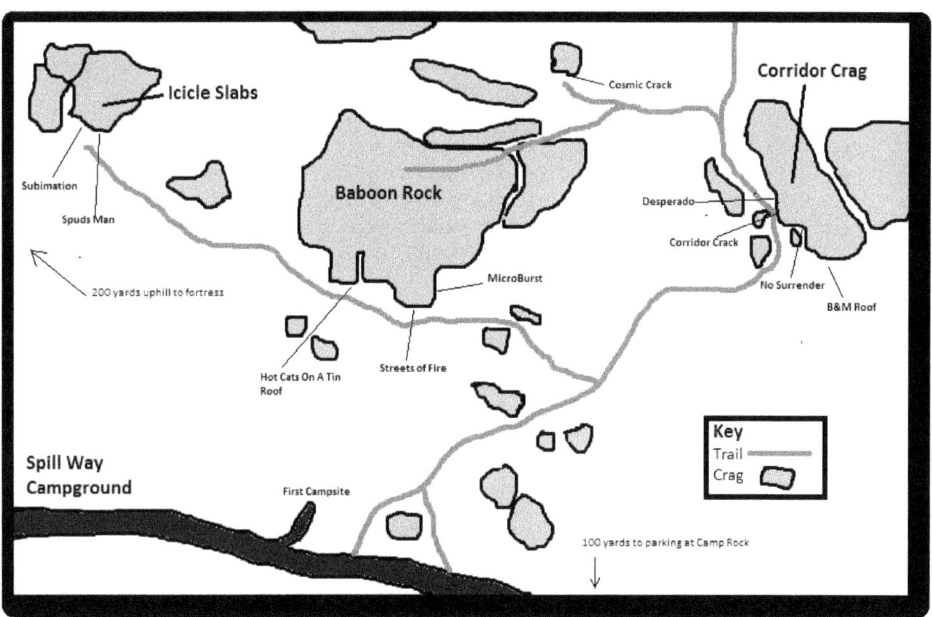

*Routes are listed from right to left…*

**A.** **B & M Roof** *5.10a* *

Thirty feet down and right of the entrance to the corridor, on the south facing side of the cliff. Take the obvious splitter hand crack through the low roof 15 feet off the ground. The crux is at the lip, which leads to much easier climbing (and worsening rock) up and right, to build a belay at the top of the cliff.
Cams to 2". No anchor. (35 feet)
*Bob D' Antonio, Richard Aschert, Dave Dangle '85*

*Atop a boulder in the small alcove…*

**B.** **No Surrender** *5.11d R* *

On top of the right boulder before the entrance to the corridor, take the right trending, overhanging flake in the center of the amphitheatre through exfoliating rock (and hard to place pro) to join a left trending, hand crack over the lip. Fun climbing, but difficult and strenuous to protect.
Cams to 3". No anchor. (35 feet)
*Bob D' Antonio, Pete Gallagher '82*

*Just inside the corridor…*

**C.** **Corridor Crack** *5.10c* **

10 feet inside the corridor, climb the obvious thin finger crack up a small bulge to another crack which leads to the top of the cliff. Quality, interesting climbing that will improve once the route has more traffic.
Nuts and cams to 2". No anchor. (45 feet)
*Andy Brown and Louise Steele '86*

**D.** **Unknown** *5.10d* *

Thirty feet left of *Corridor,* take the left trending, huge rail up to join a crack. Climb past one bolt, then angle up and right through easier, but run-out terrain over the lip.
1 bolt, Nuts and Cams to 2". No anchor. (45 feet)

*The final route is located hundred meters along the trail leading to the summit of Baboon Rock. Follow the left fork of the trail from the corridor, and head west uphill for 60 feet until some slabs can be seen up and right, past two small corridors of rock. Scramble right over the slabs, aiming for the boulder and large dead tree below the small panel. On the left side of the panel is…*

E. **Cosmic Crack** *5.9* ***

While really only a long boulder problem, this beautiful, overhanging hand crack is well worth the hike if you're in the area. Sustained jamming up perfect hands yields the summit and a small tree to belay from. Originally soloed!

Cams to 3". Tree Anchor. (25 feet)

*Mark Rolofson and Bob D'Antonio*

# Baboon Rock

*[Located above the Spillway Campground on the east hillside]*

Like a guardian statue that looks over Spillway Campground, the "Gorilla" shaped cliff hosts a fine assortment of splitter cracks as well as two good sport routes. The right side of the cliff has a lot of potential for new traditional lines, so be sure to make this your first stop when looking for first ascents!

**Approach:** Walk into Spillway Campground from the parking area down the dirt road, toward the first campsite. Before the campsite appears on your right, there is a large freestanding boulder and an obvious nature trail which cuts past the boulder on the left. Take this trail up the hill and right, until you get to a small valley. You will see the obvious Baboon Rock on your left, or continue up to the Corridor Crag on your right. There is a relatively obvious hiker's trail which forks left up to the crag. Scramble up this continually fading trail, and you will reach the cliff and the overhanging panel where *Microburst* lies. Continue east around the corner to the main alcove.

*On the left side of the alcove is a large detached pillar which hosts…*

**A.** **Unfinished Business** *5.11a* **

A decent alternate start to *Hot Cats* which offers varied, technical climbing and exciting position with moves above mostly marginal gear. Old school and hard for the grade!

**Pitch 1** (5.11a): On the left side of the pillar, take the steep hand crack (crux) out the short, overhanging roof and angle up and right following the shallow crack to join *Hot Cats* after 40 feet. Clip the old pin, and take sustained steeper climbing to the ledge that marks the top of the pillar to build an anchor.

Nuts, wires, and cams to 2". No Anchor. (85 feet)

**Pitch 2** (5.10b): Step right off the belay, across the large chimney, and head up a long left-facing, right trending dihedral to a small roof, where multiple cracks converge. Either belay here, and take a short pitch to the summit, or link it as one monster pitch (bring multiple slings!).

Small nuts and cams to 3". No anchor. (120 feet)

Full rack of nuts and cams to 3". (205 total feet)

*Kevin Patno '86*

F
G
H
E
A
B
C
D
F G
H I

B. **Hot Cats on a Tin Roof** *5.11a* *

Another decent route on the face, however it has become overgrown and flakey over the past 25 years since the first ascent. Old school and hard for the grade!
**Pitch 1** (5.11a): On the right side of the pillar, ten feet left of the strikingly obvious off-width, climb the steep crux out the short overhanging roof and angle up left following the shallow crack to clip the old pin. Take sustained, steeper climbing to the ledge that marks the top of the pillar, and build an anchor.
Nuts, wires, and cams to 2". No Anchor. (85 feet)
**Pitch 2** (5.10b): Step right off the belay, across the large chimney, and head up a long left-facing, right trending dihedral to a small roof where multiple cracks converge. Either belay here, and take a short pitch to the summit, or link it as one monster pitch (bring multiple slings!).
Small nuts and cams to 3". No anchor. (120 feet)
Full rack of nuts and cams to 3". (205 total feet)
*Jeff Rhodes and Mark Sullivan '86*

C. **The Big Peach** *5.8* *

The obvious, very difficult to protect, off-width crack in the middle of the face. Stunning position, but with no protection! Build an anchor as for *Hot Cats* and *Unfinished Business*. Leave gear to rap or finish those routes.
Big Bros, full rack of cams to 6". No anchor. (90 feet)

D. **Fly or Fry** *5.11a R/X*

Once a Gallagher classic, this crumbling, run-out pile has now drifted into obscurity. With bad protection, and bad rock, there is a reason this route sees few ascents! Old school and hard for the grade!
**Pitch 1** (5.11a R/X): To the right of the off-width, take the obvious thin seam up the middle of the face, past shrubs, loose rock, and bad pins to build a belay up and left at under-cling seams at the break. Don't fall!
3 pins, Nuts, wires, and cams to 2". No Anchor. (95 feet)
**Pitch 2** (5.10b): Step left off the belay, and take any of the obvious cracks up and right to a large, left facing, right trending dihedral. Either build a belay on the left side of the large roof, or link together the last pitches for one monster long pitch.
Small nuts and cams to 3". No anchor. (120 feet)
Full rack of nuts and cams to 3". (205 total feet)
*Jeff Rhodes and Mark Sullivan '86*

E. **Warren Route** *5.10d* ***

Great position and cool climbing! This route is probably the most popular line on the cliff, due to its obviousness on the left side of the large overhanging panel.
**Pitch 1** (5.10b): On the left side of the large overhang, take the obvious left trending, juggy crack up to build a belay at the ledge alcove.
Nuts and cams to 5". No Anchor. (70 feet)
**Pitch 2** (5.10d): Step left off the belay, and climb the obvious, beautiful, left arching crack through the dihedral, over the lip to a slab crack and a good belay stance on the left side of the large roof. The best pitch on the route!
Nuts and cams to 3". No anchor. (100 feet)

**Pitch 3** (5.9): Angle left under the roof to join a long easy crack system to the summit. Nuts and cams to 4". (80 feet)
Full rack of nuts and cams to 5". (250 total feet)
*Robert Warren and John Kato '80*

*To the right of the overhang between the two steeper panels…*

*F.* **Something's Burning** *5.11b ****

A harder and more sustained variation than *Streets*, this route is another good line for those looking for a little exposure and adventure.
**Pitch 1:** (5.10c): Easy face climbing between cracks leads up the left facing dihedral, to a lie-back crux protected by an old pin. Take the left fork in the Y crack, and jam through sustained climbing to a slab where you can build a belay below the large prominent roof.
**Pitch 2:** (5.9): Take the crack system up the right side of the roof through a brief, overhanging crux to the summit.
Nuts and Cams to 3". No anchors. (120 feet)
*Jeff Rhoads and Mike Sullivan '86*

*G.* **Streets of Fire** *5.10c ***

**Pitch 1:** (5.10c): Easy face climbing between cracks, leads up the left facing dihedral, to a lie-back crux protected by an old pin. Take the right fork of the Y crack, and jam past airy climbing over the slab to build a belay below a prominent roof (same as *Burning*).
**Pitch 2:** (5.9): Take the crack system up the right side of the roof through a brief overhanging crux to the summit.
Nuts and cams to 3". No anchors. (120 feet)
*Jeff Rhoads and Mike Sullivan '86*

*Around the corner on the east facing panel…*

*H.* **Gorilla** *5.12c ***

Good position and good rock make this a worthwhile outing. Start by fifth classing for the first 20 feet to a ledge, clip the bolt, and rock up into a hard boulder problem on crimps and slopers that deposit you at the big jug. Cut immediately up and left, making big moves between big holds. Once on the face, the technical gaston crux guards the anchors.
8 bolts. Cold-shut anchors. (60 feet)
*Dan Durland*

*I.* **MicroBurst** *5.13c ****

One of the better hard routes in the canyon, the name says it all! Start the same as *Gorilla*, but head straight up after the rest through really fun 5.12 climbing between in-cut seems to slopers below the bulge. Get composed and launch off of in-cuts via an all-points-off dyno to a sloping loaf. One more hard move guards the anchors up high. Great movement! A couple of abandoned studs are out right protecting a project, which isn't worthwhile because it keeps breaking…
8 bolts. Cold-shut anchors. (60 feet)
*Ben Schmitt and Dan Durland '10*

# Icicle Slab

*[Located 200 feet west of Baboon Rock above Spillway Campground]*

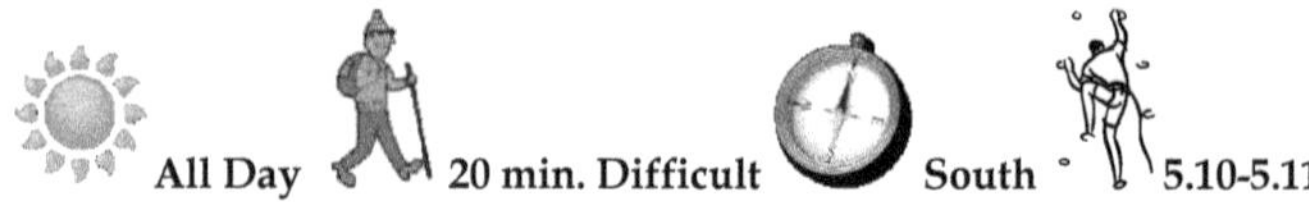


This small slab would be a decent place to check out if Baboon is too crowded.

**A.** **Sumblimation** *5.10a* **

A decent slab crack up the center of the face, climbs past a crux roof to anchors. Pitch two follows a crack system to the summit.
Nuts and Cams to 3". Chain anchor. (60 feet)
*Brian Blackstock and Rick Lince '86*

**B.** **Spuds Man** *5.11a* *

Climb the crack system to the right of *Sublimation*.
Nuts and cams to 3". Chain anchor. (60 feet)
*Dan Durland*

# The Fortress

*[Located high on the west hillside above Spillway Campground]*

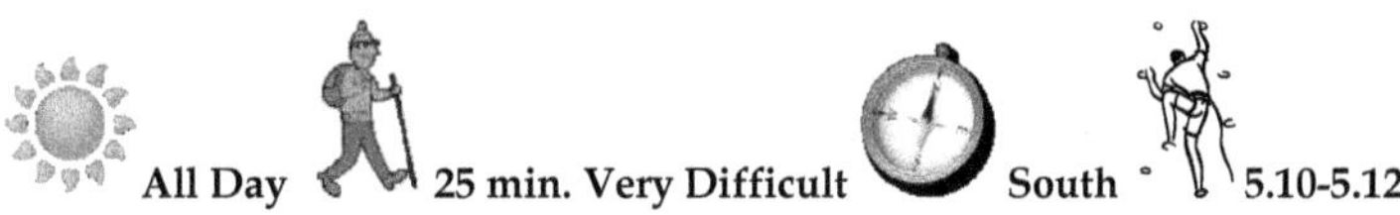


At the far end of the road, on the high hillside, north of the looming Elevenmile Dam, the Fortress is by far the most vast and expansive rock outcropping in all of Elevenmile. While not for the faint of heart, the approach is steep, and the routes are long and committing. For those who do venture up to this enormous feature, the rewards are unmatched as the solitude and views are superb. The routes developed here feel much more akin to the alpine nature of climbs on Pikes Peak, and were primarily developed in the mid 1980's and early nineties by the local Elevenmile crew of Bob D'Antonio, Richard Aschert, Neil Cannon, Dave Dangle, Mark Milligan, Jeff Rhodes, and Mike Sullivan.

**Lower Tier**
*Starting on the right side of the lower tier, routes are listed from right to left.*

**A.** **Let There Be Rock** *5.12b* **

On the far right side of the cliff, left of a large water chute on a panel relatively off by itself, this technical route climbs up the sheer face, through decent edging moves to anchors over the lip.
5 bolts. Sling Anchor. (60 feet)
*Glenn Schuler and Mark Milligan 91'*

**B.** **Canyon Classic** *5.11d* ****

The name says it all! Awesome and hard for the grade, this stellar route takes the prominent hand and fist splitter up the overhanging face in the middle of the blank panel. Crux it through the sustained bottom half, then angle up and left to finish through a juggy seam. Pumpy, involved, and dirty from years of neglect, it will clean up with more traffic. Walk off the top.
Triple cams to 4", hand and fist sizes, small stoppers. No anchor. (110 feet)
*Bob D' Antonio, Richard Aschert, Dave Dangle '85*

**C.** **Rock Busters** *5.12c* *

Up and left of *Canyon Classic,* this line takes a chossy slab past two bolts and a technical crux to a nice "dogleg" crack that angles up and left to finish up below a roof.
Cams and nuts to 3". No Anchor. (80 feet)
*Richard Aschert and Bob D' Antonio '85*

*The next two routes are located 100 feet west of Rock Busters on a small wall with two right leaning, overhanging cracks…*

**D.** **The Hurting** *5.12c R **

On a small, overhanging, triangular panel, this route takes the right seam up and left through desperate moves, hard to place gear, and mediocre rock, to build a belay on the top of the triangle. Rap from the belay stance via old webbing.
Cams and nuts to 2". No Anchor. (50 feet)
*Bob D'Antonio '85*

**E.** **Thief of Rock** *5.12b ***

Take the left seam past an old bolt through a lie-back crux, and angle up and right through sustained, flaring crack climbing to the top of the triangle. Rap from the belay stance via old webbing.
Cams and nuts to 2". No Anchor. (50 feet)
*Bob D'Antonio '85*

*60 feet west around the corner, there is a vast slab. The next route starts on the right side of the low-angle slab below a small roof above a ledge…*

**F.** **Shot on Sight** *5.10c* **

**Pitch 1:** (5.10c): Climb the stellar finger and hand crack up and right through good rock to belay at the ledge below the roof
**Pitch 2:** (5.9-5.11): Take the left crack off the ledge (called *Barbwire Fence* 5.9), or the right crack (called *Electric Fence* 5.11a) over the roof to build an anchor at the summit. Nuts and Cams to 3". No anchors. (120 feet)
*Jeff Rhoads and Mike Sullivan '86*

*In the huge, courtyard sized alcove between the major 300 foot wide dihedral, two classic routes take the south facing panel and are accessed by third classing to an obvious ledge and building a belay.*

**G.** **Vapor Drawings** *5.10d* ***

Starting on the obvious ledge, take the line of horizontal crack systems up and left of the small roof above the ledge. This is sustained edging and good technical moves past three bolts. Join a right facing dihedral comprised of double fist cracks to finish at the top of the crag. Walk off the back side of the face. Really good, varied climbing, with killer views!
3 bolts, cams and nuts to 3". No Anchor. (100 feet)
*Darryl Roth, Dave Dangle, and Richard Aschert '86*

**H.** **Bits and Pieces** *5.11c* ****

Start off the ledge and angle up right past two mini roofs to join three bolts of technical, cruxy face climbing on the arête. Cap a small bulge and angle up left, to join an overhanging finger crack (red point crux). Finish at the top of the cliff. Sustained, beautiful, and the best exposure of any climb in the canyon! Walk off the back side of the face.
3 bolts, cams and nuts to 3". No Anchor. (100 feet)
*Richard Aschert, Bob D'Antonio, and Dave Dangle '85*

www.ingramcontent.com/pod-product-compliance
Ingram Content Group UK Ltd.
Pitfield, Milton Keynes, MK11 3LW, UK
UKHW020128250726
13967UKWH00002B/534

9 781257 789337